Madison & Dane County

by Ron Seely

Managing Editor, William C. Robbins

American & World Geographic Publishing
in cooperation with
Wisconsin State Journal and
The Capital Times

For my wife, Doreen. For my children, Will and Anna. And, especially, in memory of my daughter, Katie, who was with me as I wrote.

ZANE WILLIAMS PHOTOS

Above: *Memorial Union Terrace.*
Right: *Lake Mendota boat house.*

Title page: *Wisconsin State Capitol.*

ZANE WILLIAMS PHOTO

Front cover: LARRY MAYER PHOTO
Back cover, top: LARRY MAYER PHOTO
Bottom: BOB FIRTH PHOTO

Library of Congress Cataloging-in-Publication Data
Seely, Ron
    Madison & Dane County / by Ron Seely.
        p.   cm.
    Includes bibliographical references and index.
    ISBN 1-56037-040-8
    1. Madison (Wis.)--History. 2. Madison (Wis.)--Ge-
ography. 3. Dane County (Wis.)--History. 4. Dane
County (Wis.)--Geography. I. Wisconsin state journal.
II. Capital times (Madison, Wis.) III. Title. IV. Title:
Madison and Dane County.
F587.M157S44 1993   93-23205
977.5'83--dc20

All design, editorial, and typesetting completed in the USA. Printed in Hong Kong by Flying Colors of Beverly Hills, CA.

ZANE WILLIAMS

Contents

The Setting	*4*
A Summer Stroll	*18*
The History	*24*
The Black Hawk War	*30*
The Workplace	*42*
Institutions and Ideas	*46*
An Architect's Legacy	*60*
Dane County	*62*
The People	*74*
The Future	*98*
Epilogue	*106*
For Further Reading	*107*
Index	*110*

BRUCE FRITZ

Above: *Looking toward Blue Mounds.*
Top: *Krista Williams in Norwegian dress.*

The Setting

Above: *The peace of day's end on a Dane County farm.*

Facing page: *Madison from the air.*

I moved to Wisconsin and to Madison in the fall, during an October that was as beautiful and as clear and as bright with color as any I had known. It was cool in the mornings and evenings and all day the air seemed deliciously clean and sharp-edged, like the transparent, shining water sluicing over the sand and rocks in the bottom of a fine trout stream.

I bought a pickup truck; it seemed the sensible thing to do. I had been hired as a reporter on the state desk of the *Wisconsin State Journal.* My editor was Steve Hopkins—a man as adept with a flyrod or an ax as with a pen, who carried the faint smell of woodsmoke always about him—and he told me that the best thing I could do was go out and get lost in the country. So I did.

I'll never forget all of that Wisconsin countryside, spread out before me like a dream. I could hardly believe my good fortune. I bumped about Dane County like a pinball, nosing around in delightful little towns with curious, earthy names like Cross Plains and Blue Mounds and Sun Prairie and Black Earth. I drove the twisting backroads, opened my pickup window and breathed in great gulps of air tangy with the aroma of drying oak leaves, turned up the country music on my radio. I frequented Main Street cafes and ate chili and drank black coffee and listened to the gossip of the small towns. In the late afternoons, homeward bound, I looked for soaring hawks above the meadows and white-tail deer grazing at wood's edge, and I stopped, happily, for farmers in rubber boots and bib overhauls who herded their Holsteins across the pavement toward red dairy barns. This human element, too, was part of the Wisconsin countryside's gentle charm; it was lived-in country, years removed from wilderness but not so tame that, at night, when great horned owls hooted and whippoorwills called, you couldn't feel a touch of wildness still there. Fishing in the early evening on a trout stream like Black Earth Creek just west of Madison you could lose yourself in the dark, fast-running water between alder-tangled banks and forget entirely that you were in settled country until, walking out of a break, you stepped onto soft, plowed earth and saw, across the field, a farmstead

LARRY MAYER

with its oaks and its barn and its wide-porched house with the lights yellow and welcoming in the dusk. It was a good feeling.

Presiding over all this countryside was the gleaming city of Madison. Sometimes, if my work kept me in the country into the night, I'd drive toward the city and, now and then, catch a glimpse of the great illuminated dome of the State Capitol. It shined like a beacon and marked the heart of the city and the state and, always, driving back on those autumnal evenings I'd look forward eagerly to my first view of the dome from some distant rise of land outside the city. The glow of the Capitol and the loom of the city's lights above it symbolized, for me, all of the city's mystery and sophistication and poetry.

When I wasn't in the countryside, I was in the city, prowling and looking and taking it all in. It was a wonderful place, a rowdy, bustling, hustling place. I walked the old neighborhoods, places like Williamson Street east of the Capitol Square, known fondly by all as Willy Street. It's a charismatic hodgepodge of a street lined by wood frame houses with comfortable, sometimes listing, porches

and is the domain of a 1960ish collection of tattoo artists, fortune tellers, avant-garde artists, and other, assorted free spirits. Along the street you'll find one of the city's best food cooperatives, a pawn shop, and a popular playhouse squeezed into a converted garage.

More often than not, I found myself drawn to the high Capitol Square with its view of the lakes, and State Street with its coffee shops and bookstores, and at the far end of State, the University of Wisconsin with its own cast of characters. There, too, were the sloping, tree-shaded expanse of Bascom Hill and cavernous Memorial Union with its fieldstone terrace out back and its oaks and its view over Lake Mendota and the yellow and orange steel tables where you could sit and drink from cold pitchers of beer you had ordered at the outside window.

In these places, around the Square and up and down State, Madison had the feel of an urban landscape; buses cruised and came to hissing halts at curbside, the occasional panhandler worked a corner, young and cocky boys lugged blaring boom boxes. On campus, taped to light posts,

were fliers advertising foreign movies and lectures by the famous and near-famous and once-famous. On the Square, beneath the Capitol dome, the dim and cool marbled corridors buzzed with political power and, on days when the state Legislature was in session, clumps of suited politicians and lobbyists clustered in the hallways talking conspiratorially.

Yet the countryside never seemed far away. This, it seemed to me, was Madison's greatest charm and the thing that lay at the heart of its character. Standing in the Capitol rotunda on a warm fall afternoon you could look far down any of the dark corridors and see through the propped-open doors the blue of the lakes or the green of the landscape, the hills with their tufts of oaks and, at the far end of State Street, the grass and the over-arching trees of Bascom Hill.

From very early on, the pastoral quality of this gentle Wisconsin landscape has touched travelers in a special way. A cranky English geologist named George W. Featherstonaugh passed through Madison in 1837 when there was little more than a log cabin tavern and the camps of the Winnebagoes. Uncharacteristically, he practically gushed in his journal, calling the future site of Madison "one of the most exquisitely beautiful regions I have ever seen in any part of the world."

Featherstonaugh was particularly taken by the park-like qualities of the countryside and wrote of the "inimitable grace with which the picturesque clumps of trees, that sometimes enlarged themselves into woods, embellished this rural landscape."

In 1845, according to Madison historian David Mollenhoff, settler H.A. Tenney and another traveler topped a rise on their way to the village of Madison one evening about sunset and were frozen by the beauty of the scene below them. "When we reached the summit," Tenney wrote, "both stopped our horses in involuntary surprise. Four Lakes (the area's Indian name) lay spread out before us, brought out in strong relief by the declining sun just sinking in the west, shining like burnished mirrors. On all sides forest and prairie swept down in lines and patches unobstructed to their shores. Except the village, magnified a thousand fold as a central figure, there

was no break in the scene—not a mark of human improvement. As this line of white beach sand glowing in the sunset stood in contrast with the dark, green foliage that encompassed it, plain and level, precipice and peninsula, bay and gulf, were clothed in a brilliancy of outline, and a beauty beyond the power of description."

It has been 15 years since I settled in Madison and, to this day, I feel the same thrill of surprise and discovery, the same sense of having found someplace different and wonderful, whenever I see the Capitol's glinting dome or the shining reach of Lake Mendota from Observatory Drive. Though I grew up in the plains of central Illinois where the horizons are flat and distant, the summer nights soft and lit by fireflies, the sunsets breathtaking, I now consider Madison and Dane County my home. I feel that this is where I belong, in these green hills and on the shores of these marshes and lakes. I have developed a sense of place, of rootedness, of deep attachment and belonging.

I am not alone in this feeling. And that, more than anything else, is what this book is

about—the unusually strong sense of belonging to this particular landscape and to this unique cityscape that characterizes the people who have lived here through the years and who call it home today. It is an extraordinary thing.

A few years ago I did a newspaper story about a reunion of UW-Madison campus activists. These were the people who had led and participated in the massive anti-war protests that surged back and forth across the campus in the late 1960s and early 1970s—protests that, in fact, helped change America's course. The protestors, now nearing middle age, had spread across the country pursuing careers in law, journalism, business, and a host of other fields. For many, the ardor and stridency of the protest years had tempered and softened and changed into a well-honed social conscience. But just about everyone I talked to retained something else from those years—a deep affection for Madison. In Los Angeles and in Washington, D.C., and in several other cities, I found displaced Madisonians who had carried something of the city with them and who longed to come back. In those two cities, I discovered, there

Above: *Across Capitol Square.*

Facing page: *A mallard enjoys Madison's close-to-nature setting.*

were even organized groups of former Madison dwellers who met now and then to trade Madison news and gossip and to reminisce about the place they all considered home.

Another example: A couple I have known for some time had led an adventurous life in their twenties, living in tents and cabins in California and Colorado and studying Buddhism for a year in India before settling, finally, in Madison with several Buddhist friends. After living here for a number of years and parenting three children, they relocated to a suburb of Washington, D.C. But the Madison bug had bitten them. For nearly three years, they remained in the east but their letters were filled with memories of Madison's blue lakes and leisurely pace and mild summer days; whenever we talked they spoke of their longing to return to the city they now knew was home. My family and I visited one summer and found a photograph of Madison's nighttime skyline—it had been given them as a gift when they left the city—displayed prominently on a wall.

Finally, after three years, they could take it no longer. My friend gave up his lucra-tive job in Washington, D.C. and the family returned. They settled on the city's wooded west side in a comfortable, wide-eaved home with a fireplace and shiny wood floors and a birch tree outside the front window. Within weeks they were back into the Madison routine of soccer games with the kids, farmer's market on Saturday morning, Lake Mendota beaches on hot Sunday afternoons. They swear they'll never leave again.

There is something about this city and this Wisconsin countryside, something about it that gets inside people.

There are writers and philosophers who have studied this. Here in Wisconsin, in particular, the strong ties be-tween the people and the landscape have given rise to an eloquent and inspiring body of literature that ponders the importance of place in our lives.

Wisconsin writer Ben Logan captured the sacredness of this land in his elegiac book *The Land Remembers,* a poignant account of his boyhood on a Wisconsin farm. Though it takes place in the unglaciated region of southwestern Wisconsin, many who love Madison and Dane County's hills and lakes will recognize the sentiment.

Logan started his book this way: "Once you have lived on the land, been a partner with its moods, secrets, and seasons, you cannot leave. The living land remembers, touching you in unguarded moments, saying, 'I am here. You are part of me.'

"When this happens to me, I go home again, in mind or in person, back to a hilltop world in southwestern Wisconsin... I was born there, cradled by the land, and I am always there even though I have been a wanderer."

William Cronon, a professor of history at the University of Wisconsin in Madison, has spent much of his career considering the role that place and the land play in our lives. He is particularly well suited to explore the relationship between the people of this part of Wisconsin and the land on which they live. He grew up in Madison, went to school at the University of Wisconsin, and went on to become a Rhodes Scholar and a professor at Yale. He returned to Madison and the University of Wisconsin to assume the prestigious Frederick Jackson Turner chair in the university's history department.

In an essay called "Landscape and Home: Environmental Traditions in Wisconsin," Cronon points out that "Wisconsin has had an especially rich tradition of people who have committed themselves to the land in a passionate and self-reflective way....

"I didn't realize how pervasive this was, until I moved away. I had grown up surrounded by friends and teachers who were just as fascinated by the land and its stories as I was. At James Madison Memorial High School, my fellow students shared my enthusiasm for learning about geology, ecology, and environmental change. At the University of Wisconsin, I found professors who raised environmental questions about their subjects regardless of whether they taught botany or geography or history or medieval sciences. Everyone around me thought it quite natural to begin their work by recognizing that people live upon the earth, so that the history of land and our place upon it was crucial no matter what the subject."

Cronon was shocked to discover that the scholarly communities at Oxford and Yale did not share such a landscape tradition.

"For them," he wrote, "environmental history was an interesting but rather eccentric subject, well outside the mainstream of their concerns.

A sense of place didn't seem nearly so important to them, or had mainly to do with buildings and the things that had happened inside them."

Why are the people of Wisconsin different? Why does a special landscape—like Madison's splendid lakes and her green hills—work its way so deeply into peoples' lives?

Cronon speculates that it is partly the way the land looks here; it is not a spectacular wilderness landscape overwhelming in its scale and beauty, he points out, but is instead a "working landscape," where woods and farms and small towns are interwoven so people are reminded that, no matter how urban we become, the land is always there, providing food and a life for creatures other than ourselves. We are never far from farms in this state, he continues, and just about everybody either hunts or knows somebody who hunts. And the land keeps reminding us of things. The moraines and drumlins remind us of the glaciers that shaped the countryside. The young, successional forests remind us of how our predecessors on the land so changed its appearance by cutting the pine forests and the oaks and turning

Summer on Lake Mendota.

over its prairies. The eutrophication of the lakes—like Mendota and Monona in Madison—reminds us of how we humans can so speed up the earth's natural processes.

"Everywhere," Cronon writes, "we see signs that the histories of land and people are bound together."

Few people have a deeper understanding of this relationship than glacial geologists. Because Madison and Dane County owe so much of their appearance to the glaciers, I figured any exploration of this special place would have to begin with at least a brief look at how these

massive sheets of ice bulldozed their way across the land 10,000 years ago. John Attig and Lee Clayton, glacial geologists with the Wisconsin Geological and Natural History Survey, do this kind of thing for a living. To them, glaciers remain as real as they were when they were scouring the Wisconsin countryside.

I arranged to spend a day with Attig and Clayton, traveling the route the last glacier took across Dane County and Madison, peeling back the earth and looking for the landscape's geological bones. I met the geologists on an April

morning on a day that promised to be warm and distinctly unglacier-like. We wore boots and jeans and the car was filled with glacial maps and a jumble of clanking shovels and pick-axes. Leaving the converted grocery store on Madison's west side that serves as the survey's office, Attig explained we would be traveling country shaped by the last major glacial episode; it was called the Wisconsin Glaciation because it was first extensively studied in this state. The glacier, born of climatic changes, moved out of east-central Canada and spread across much of North

BRENT NICASTRO

Above: *Yahara Place Park.*

Facing page: *Catch of the day in Dane County.*

America. In Wisconsin, the glacier reached its southern-most point, just south of what is now Dane County, about 15,000 years ago. This part of Wisconsin was covered by an arm of the glacier called the Green Bay Lobe.

Geologists, I discovered, are drawn to road cuts and to gravel pits, places where the insides of the earth are laid bare and where they can best do their own special kind of divining. The naturalist John Muir, raised not far away on a farm near Portage, called the messages that can be read in such places "rock scrip-tures." We made our first stop at a road cut just south of the Dane County village of Waunakee, about ten miles north of Madison. There, At-tig and Clayton used their shovels to slice away at the ragged hillside exposing lay-ers of earth laid down hun-dreds of millions years ago by the waves of an ancient lake. The land was once much higher here, Attig said, but was sheared and leveled by the glaciers and then topped by the dust and dirt that was kicked up by the wind blow-ing off the cold glacier's sur-face. He waved to the gently sloping hills around us, all about the same height and all

plowed farm fields. Much of eastern Dane County looks the same. Were it 10,000 years ago, Attig said, we'd be about ten miles inside the gla-cier, buried beneath 400 feet of ice.

We drove, the rest of the morning, down what used to be the sloping face of an an-cient glacier site that Attig made real with his running commentary. At a gravel pit just north of Madison, Clay-ton cut into a steep wall with his shovel and exposed, for the first time in thousands of years, a striated band of earth laid down by the glacier. With quick, deft strokes of the shovel's blade, Clayton sliced away layer after thin layer of the earth and, suddenly, we were watching the pages of a strange and ancient flip book; we could see, in the undulat-ing striations of earth, the mud and sand actually oozing from beneath the glacier to flow and move ahead of the great, shearing mass of ice. Clayton speculated that here, because of the odd way the glacial till is distributed, the glacier had formed a delta, dumping its debris into an-cient Lake Yahara, the sweeping body of water that would eventually become Madison's four lakes.

Later, just a few miles south and west of Madison, we hiked along the Johnstown Moraine, the wooded ridge that marks the southernmost point of the glacier's advance. Some 15,000 years ago, Attig said, we would have been standing in the cool shadow of a 200-foot wall of ice. There would have been wind blowing off the cold face of the glacier and flowing wa-ter and tumbling, rolling rocks and stones. There would have been sharp reports, almost like thunder at times, as the brittle and moving ice cracked. The glacier would have sloped up and away to the north, Attig said, "a long, dizzying, rising white plain." To the south would have stretched frozen, treeless tundra.

Today, from atop Johnstown Moraine, the lega-cy left us by the glacier is easy to see and to appreciate. Immediately south and west of the moraine, in country that escaped the glacier's force, the land was folded and creased and wooded; to the north lay dark and rolling farm fields, freshly plowed and ready to plant. To some, Attig said, the glaciers may be ancient history, but we modern-day humans still live our lives—still build our homes and villages and plant

Tenney Park Lagoon.

Right: *Maypole dance at the dedication of the CUNA world head-quarters, May 31, 1980.*
Below: *Room with a view.*

John Attig

our fields and construct our roads—in the places the glaciated landscape tells us to.

So now I sit at my writing desk thinking about all of these things, this ancient ground beneath me and this old home where I live and the years I have spent in this place, this neighborhood, this city. The writer Wallace Stegner wrote that a place does not truly become a place until it has been profoundly touched by its inhabitants, until it has seen births and deaths and joy and tragedy, the passing of time and the slow accrual of human history, piling up like coral on an ocean reef. I have only lived in this Madison neighborhood for 15 years; that is an invisible blip in the eyes of my friends the geologists. Yet I have started piling up the history here, making my place.

I have reached middle age here. I have known happiness in this place and great sadness. I have come to know and appreciate all of those large and small things that add up to knowing, really knowing, exactly where I am in the world. It is spring as I write this and there are things I have come to expect about this season in this Wis-

consin place and in this Madison house. I know that every spring about this time, the lilacs outside the window above my desk will bloom and fill the house with their perfume. I know that, a few weeks later, the tall locust trees will flower and that, within days, the fragrant petals of the flowers will float down like snowflakes across our yard and our driveway. I know that for a week or two every year about this time, I can enjoy the sweet trill of the white-throated sparrow and I know that I must appreciate it while I can because it pauses here only shortly on its northern migratory route.

As much as I feel a part of such seasonal changes, I have also come to know about those larger natural cycles that shaped this corner of the earth. I know now from the geologists that I can walk down the wooded slope behind my house and find potholes left by the glacier and rocks and boulders that bear the glacier's signature. I know that the glacier covered my backyard about 10,000 years ago and that,

thousands of years hence, it will cover it again.

All of these things make this place what it is, and knowing these things have made me a part of this place. I have become what the writer Wendell Berry calls a "placed" person.

A few years ago I decided to cease thinking about making any further career moves, to tear up my resume, to be content with where I have arrived in my career and in my life, to do my job well and to live well, to settle in this house, on the shoulder of this hill, in this good city of Madison. Some might consider this a bad thing, a kind of surrender to the passing years and to conservative middle age. But I find comfort and peace in the decision and in knowing that I'll be able to link my own days to the life of this place, to the coming and going of the ice from the city's lakes, the hatching of mayflies on the trout streams outside of town, the blooming of the wild columbine beside my doorstep where it has grown from the familiar Wisconsin earth.

17

A Summer Stroll

Grace Episcopal Church and farmer's market.

Madison, with its high, glacier-sculpted isthmus and its tree-shaded lakes and its old and interesting neighborhoods, is a fine place to walk.

And there is no finer time to begin your walk than a summer Saturday morning when the sun is just coming up above the marshes north and east of the city and, on the Capitol Square where the sloping lawns are still wet with dew, the farmers are unloading their produce from their trucks beneath the big and dark-leafed oaks and carrying wooden crates heavy with vegetables to their curbside stands in preparation for the weekly farmer's market.

A good place to start is the Cafe Europa on the southeast corner of the Square. The cafe is in a high, triangular stone building with an old-world look to it and wide windows with cloth awnings above them and, inside, plenty of tables where you can sit and sip the dark, rich coffees they serve there. But on a clear and bright early summer morning, the best place to be is at a table outside on the sidewalk. There you can enjoy the coolness of the hour before the heat of the day, and

Right: *Farmer's market.*
Below: *Along State Street.*

smell the concrete city still fresh from the night and, sitting at one of the tables beneath the flowering trees, you can look east and see the sun coming up behind the church steeples or you can look west toward the Capitol dome that is burnished gold with the sun's rising. The first and earliest sounds of the farmer's market will drift across East Hamilton to your table: the slamming of pickup doors and the shouts of the market workers as they prepare for the day.

You can order your second cup of coffee to go and carry it warm in your hand across the street to the market where early shoppers browse, looking for the freshest offerings. Before you plunge into the crowd, give a nod to the statue of gallant Colonel Hegg at the corner of East Hamilton and Pinckney Streets. Born in Norway, he fell fighting for the Union on September 9, 1862 on the bloody fields of Chickamauga in the Civil War. Now the shadow of his statue provides shade for cardtables on summer Saturday mornings set up around the big, square base and weighted with literature from all manner of just causes—from animal activist groups to nuclear freeze campaigns. Once past the Colonel you can study the vegetables or you can study the people. Have a seat on a bench or on the lawn and finish your coffee. Who said you had to walk on a walk? It will, probably, be the standard Madison crowd—sandalled and tennis-shoed, lots of cotton, a goodly number of tie-dye Ts, Lycra biking shorts, plenty of chinos, dogs on leashes with bandannas around their necks, reusable shopping bags made from canvas and nylon mesh.

The farmers will be singing the praises of their offerings. In the late spring there are bags of earthy morel mushrooms, the dirt from rural Wisconsin's forested hillsides clinging to them. They are as prized as jewels in season—try them rolled in flour and lightly pan-fried to a crispy golden brown—and have been known to fetch as much as $12 a pound. Perhaps you will stroll by the table manned by Matthew Smith, a lanky and smiling farmer with a long, red pony tail who will sell you thick, green spears of fragrant asparagus from his hill-side farm in western Dane County. Or maybe you'll buy wild rice from the bearded fellow up the street whose nearby truck seems to permanently wear a canoe, like a bonnet. If you have a spot of coffee left, buy a Danish or a muffin or a thick slice of pumpkin bread. If you need energy, save your money for the fudge cart on the northwest corner of the Square.

By the time you have torn yourself away from the temptations of the market, the stores along the outer rim of the Square and up and down State Street will be opening their doors. You can admire original wildlife prints at the Stanton & Lee Gallery on Mifflin Street or leaf through thousands of second-hand books at Shakespeare's Bookstore on the west side of the Square, where the pine bookshelves still smell freshly cut and the titles are many and varied.

Walk down State Street then, pausing for a look up the street toward green and sloping Bascom Hill on the University of Wisconsin campus and perhaps back at the shining dome of the Capitol. If you have time duck into the

State Historical Society of Wisconsin museum on your left or the Children's Museum on your right or the Veteran's Museum or, a little farther down, the Madison Civic Center where you can check out the latest art or photography exhibit and see which of any number of national and international traveling shows is coming to town.

It is impossible to walk up State Street without stopping. You can linger at dozens of shops on the way, admiring everything from original African masks to Asian pottery to hand-woven South American sweaters. There are bookstores and pet stores and skateboard shops and stylish catalog outlet stores. There are art galleries and soap and perfume shops and half a dozen music stores and a wonderful second-hand clothing store called Ragstock.

The people you will encounter will be almost as diverse; people of every race and nationality—teenagers with orange mohawks, college kids weaving through traffic on rollerblades, young couples with strollers, a neighborhood police officer walking the beat. There will be street musicians and panhandlers and magicians and sidewalk merchants selling everything from jewelry to flowers.

By lunch time you'll be ready to sit and there are plenty of sidewalk cafes where you can enjoy the passing parade while dining on everything from fast food to gourmet meals. If you wait until you get to the University of Wisconsin campus at the far end of State Street, you can, for not much money, buy lunch from a number of food carts that do business on the concrete expanse known as Library Mall. Take your plate up onto the thick grass of Bascom Hill and enjoy the view back down State toward the Capitol dome.

Once you've finished, a nap in the grass would probably be in order, especially if the sun is shining down and mixing with the soft city noises from the street below. If you're in the mood to continue exploring, head north to the Memorial Union. Walk through the building's cool, marble interior to the Rathskeller with its arched entryways and delightful murals. Pass on through to the back of the building and out the doors to one of the city's real treasures—the Memorial Union Terrace. Here, beneath the spreading branches of old oaks, are brightly painted tables and chairs scattered across a fieldstone terrace and overlooking the blue spread of Lake Mendota and its hazy green northern shore. It is such a pleasant place you'll be tempted to order from the Union's extensive beer selections and watch the white sails out on the lake or, perhaps, listen to the jazz or the reggae band that may be playing on the outdoor stage.

If you are ambitious, the lake beckons. There are sailboats and canoes and rowboats to be rented, or there is a wooded trail that follows the Mendota campus shoreline to the west. Follow it out to distant Picnic Point and back and you'll probably return to the Union in time for the sunset and then, after dusk, when the lights of the city are beginning to shine, you can walk out to the end of the swimming pier, dangle your feet in the cool water, and marvel at the sense of wildness that the big, dark lake still lends to this northern city.

Left: *Memorial Union,*
University of Wisconsin.
Below: *Madison Civic Center.*
State Street.

Facing page: *Memorial Union*
Terrace from Lake Mendota.

The History

...there is clear evidence of the power of these lakes and this country to draw and hold people, to give them a home and a sense of place and belonging in the landscape.

About 12,000 years ago the first human beings followed the cold, receding wall of the last, great glacier into what is now Dane County. They're called Early Paleo-Indians; they were the ancestors of today's Native Americans.

What brought them into this country is time's mystery. These people were hunters and gatherers, so perhaps they were drawn by game; mammoths and mastodon were here then: giant beaver, caribou, and bison. Or maybe, even in those distant times, humans felt compelled to see what was over the next hill. Maybe, curious, they simply wanted to take a look around. Standing on a rise of land west of the present city, they would have looked upon a landscape much different from the one we travel about in today. The lakes were there, but in rough outline only, buried beneath enormous glacial Lake Yahara. The lake was strewn with islands, including a band curving across the lake where the city's famous isthmus is today. There were grasslands and dark stands of spruce and fir. To the north was a belt of tundra leading to the icy edge of the glacier.

It was, apparently, fine country—even then. Archaeologists have discovered the distinctive long and fluted spearpoints of the Early Paleo-Indians in greater quantities in Dane County than anywhere else in the state. Such spearpoints have been discovered mostly at campsites along the Yahara River and around the lake shores.

By 5000 B.C., with the Northern Hemisphere having slowly warmed over the previous thousands of years, the landscape that would eventually be the site of Madison started looking more like it does today. The conifer forests were replaced by stands of oak and hickory with their rich undergrowth. There were broader stretches of prairie. And people continued to find this a good place to live, to be drawn by the richness of the food the land offered and by its beauty. The Late Archaic people, between 3000 and 1000 B.C., had a satisfying diet of deer and wild turkey and numbers of migratory birds, fish and shellfish from the streams and lakes, and nuts and other vegetable foods from the forests. Their camps were built on the lakeshores and on rises above the county's broad marshes; dozens of the sites have been dis-

Madison in 1867.

covered in over half of the county's townships, including ten around Nine Springs Marsh and Lake Waubesa.

The Indian settlements remained and grew over the centuries and the people changed with the times; they started working copper, using tobacco and making pipes, hunting with bows and arrows, growing corn. Around 300 A.D. a fascinating culture called the Effigy Mound Tradition arose, its society built around the construction of animal-shaped earthen mounds for worship and for burial. Many of these mounds remain today, mysterious turtles and birds and bears upon the modern landscape, testament to the sacredness of this place to an ancient people.

It remains unclear what Native American tribes were settled in the area when the first French traders and explorers came through in the 1600s. The Foxes and the Sauks—two of several tribes forced into Wisconsin as the Iroquois expanded their eastern empire—had large settlements at Prairie du Sac and Blue Mounds and may have controlled the Four Lakes area. But by the time the first settlers built their cabins, members of the indigenous Winnebago tribe were living comfortably in villages around the lakes; they called the country *Taychoperah* or Four Lakes. It was the Winnebagoes who ceded the territory to the U.S. government in 1832. Early settlers found them living in haystack-shaped huts that were covered with rushes and birch bark. They paddled birchbark canoes at surprising speeds across the lakes, grew bushels and bushels of corn, harvested wild rice, and engaged happily in spare-time pursuits like footraces and wrestling. After ceding their lands, the Winnebagoes were moved

25

University of Wisconsin residence halls.

by government troops to camps west of the Mississippi but many later returned to the state to settle near Black River Falls and Wisconsin Dells. Drawn by memories of their homelands around Madison's lakes and the good life they had there, they would make seasonal pilgrimages through the years to the sites of their former villages. And well into the 1900s, residents of Monona recalled the Winnebagoes selling their baskets near the intersection of Bridge Road and Highways 12 and 18.

From all of these countless years of prehistory and early history, we are left with frustratingly little in the way of historical record; we've pieced together what we can from stone tools and weapons, from ceremonial mounds and burial sites, from the scant archaeological debris of campsites. But even from this, there is clear evidence of the power of these lakes and this country to draw and hold people, to give them a home and a sense of place and belonging in the landscape. Over tens of thousands of years, the archaeologists tell us, people came here and built their shelters next to the lakes and on the high ground above the marshes where they could look out across the distance and see the cattails and the sun glinting silver on the water's surface and the overwhelming openness of the skies filled in those long-ago days with sweeping, breathtaking skeins of geese and ducks and all manner of wild fowl. And from their campsites, too, they must have felt the wildness and the strangeness of the hills and the forests beyond—from which, at night, came the screaming of giant cats and the howl of wolves. It was, then, a wilderness that we'll never know again and that we can only dimly sense today in a silent, remnant patch of prairie in the county's southern reaches

Sunrise on Lake Monona.

or, perhaps, in the shadows of the marshes along the Wisconsin River to the north where the ages-old call of the sandhill crane can still be heard in the cold, early spring.

Among the early European explorers and passers-through, a few put down in words their sense that the Four Lakes country was an exceptional place. One of the earliest descriptions comes from a lead miner named Ebeneezer Brigham. He passed through in the summer of 1828 while traveling between Fort Winnebago at Portage and his lead mine on the southern border of what would become Dane County. He arrived on the isthmus between Lakes Mendota and Monona late in the afternoon and set up a tent of blankets near the top of the hill on which the State Capitol now sits. Resting at his campsite that evening, perhaps enjoying a pipe and surveying the wilderness and the lakes around him, he was struck by what he called "the strange beauty of the place." Later he described the isthmus to a local historian as being "an open prairie on which grew a few dwarf oaks, while thickets covered the lower grounds."

Governor James Duane Doty.

Brigham was so impressed with what he saw that afternoon and evening that he predicted a city would grow up on the beautiful spot; it might even be, Brigham said, that a city in such a rare setting could become the capital of a state. Later, Brigham would settle in the city he had foreseen, and he would die in Madison, too. By the time of his death, thirty-three years after his night among the oaks of the wild and unsettled isthmus, a domed state capitol stood on his former campsite.

The same summer Brigham traveled across the isthmus, another man eventually even more influential in the city's founding also passed between Lakes Mendota and Monona and noted the area's beauty. Judge James Doty, a Michigan judge serving the territory called Wisconsin, was mak-

ing one of several trips between Green Bay and Prairie du Chien. He presided over courts in both cities and normally made the trip by canoe on the Fox-Wisconsin water route. But on this trip he went by land to look over the new country; it was a decision that changed his future and forever linked him to the city that would be called Madison. Although there is no record of his impressions from that first journey through the Four Lakes country, Doty, based on his later role in the city's founding, must have been quite taken with what he saw.

It wasn't until late in 1834, after the brief but bloody Black Hawk War, that the future site of Madison was entered into the federal government's survey books. The surveyor, a fellow named Orson Lyon, started his work on a Friday, December 4, and surveyed on Sunday what would become the Capitol Square. He worked in near wilderness, noting Indian trails and using as his bearing-trees enormous old hickories, burr-oaks, and white oaks, and recording in field notes the sweep of the lakes that he could see as he worked, which stretched

The view west from the capitol up State Street toward the University of Wisconsin in 1897.

away on either side of the high isthmus.

Less than a year after the completion of the survey, a land office opened in Green Bay, and among the parcels of land put up for sale were those atop the Four Lakes isthmus; the asking price was $1.25 an acre. Surprisingly, the isthmus land remained unsold for five months—an irony that would be quickly recognized by any business person trying to negotiate a lease on isthmus property today. When the first of the land was sold, it was bought by none other than Doty, the former judge, who had be-

come the western land agent for several wealthy eastern land speculators. Eventually, Doty gained control of nearly the entire isthmus, including the site of the future capitol. In October of 1836, en route to the village of Belmont west of the Four Lakes country where the Territorial legislature was in session, Doty and J.V. Suydam, a surveyor he had employed, stopped on the isthmus to measure lots and draw the plat of a city. It was not a new task for him; working as a land agent for the wealthy fur magnate John Jacob Astor, he had laid out other cities in the territory, in-

cluding Green Bay and Fond du Lac. But he was particularly enthusiastic as he directed the work of his surveyor on the isthmus that October. Doty had grand plans for the high piece of green wilderness with its blue lakes. The men worked for three days, staying each night in the log cabin of a French trader named Michael St. Cyr. When they finished, they left immediately for Belmont where the most important piece of business on the Territorial legislature's agenda was the selection of a new state capital.

In Belmont, Doty put the

The Black Hawk War

Traveling into and across Madison, from the far southeast corner of the city and along the northern shore of Lake Monona and on up across the Ishtmus and then along Lake Mendota's wooded shoreline, you'll come across a series of stone monuments that mark one of the city's sadder, bloodier moments.

Along the route marked by the monuments, during the warm days of July 1832, the proud and defiant Sauk chief Black Hawk led 1,000 of his starving band, including many women and children and elderly, on a desparate march to the Mississippi. They were pursued by 3,000 U.S. militiamen led by General Henry Atkinson.

Just a few months before, Black Hawk had defied an order from the U.S. government to abandon the Sauks' ancestral homelands along the Mississippi River in northern Illinois and relocate west of the river in Iowa. Black Hawk led his band across the river from Iowa in April 1832 with the intention of settling again at the tribe's summer camp along the Rock River to raise corn for the season. But he was met by U.S. soldiers.

When he tried to surrender, inexperienced U.S. militiamen misconstrued the attempt as an attack and in the ensuing skirmish, one of the Sauks was killed. The next day the angry Sauks launched a number of attacks on outposts on the northwestern Illinois frontier.

For several months afterward, Black Hawk and his followers hid in the marshes of northern Illinois and southern Wisconsin; there were many deaths, especially among the elderly, because of the poor diet of grass, roots, and bark. In late May, Black Hawk started leading his people toward the Mississippi. Atkinson's soldiers picked up Black Hawk's trail almost by accident and the final, bloody pursuit was begun.

The soldiers caught up with stragglers at the rear of Black Hawk's band in mid-July on Madison's Isthmus, which was not yet settled and remained grown up in vegetation so thick that, according to one of the militia's scouts, you could not see another man ten steps away. On Saturday, July 21, after breaking their camp on the north shore of Lake Monona, the soldiers started their bloodthirsty march across the Isthmus.

Their first victim was an elderly Indian they discovered huddling in the underbrush. The man was "popped on the spot," by a Dr. Addison Philleo, the regimental surgeon who was also editor of the newspaper in Galena. Philleo's role in the Black Hawk War, judging from the stories told about him in the journals of other soldiers, was particularly heartless and gruesome. After shooting the elderly Indian, who had not made any threatening gesture or even tried to defend himself, Philleo grabbed the Indian's knife and proceeded to take the scalp from the man's head. The pain partially revived the Indian who groaned, whereupon Philleo said, "If you don't like being scalped with a dull knife, why didn't you keep a better one?"

Later, according to the journal kept by Surgeon's Mate John Wakefield, "another sick or disabled Indian who begged for quarter was shot by Dr. Philleo during the pursuit." Black Hawk's band had spent the night behind a hastily-erected breastworks on top of Bascom Hill. But as

Wisconsin River at Sand City.

ZANE WILLIAMS

the soldiers drew nearer on Saturday, they moved to the west and north toward the Wisconsin River near Sauk City. As part of the group tried to cross the river there, the band's warriors turned to fight. The battle lasted into the evening.

On the night of Sunday, July 22, Black Hawk tried once again to surrender. He crept near the militia camp, climbed a tree, and spoke loudly into the night, using Winnebago in the hopes that some of the Winnebagoes traveling with the soldiers would understand him. Long into the night, he shouted his plea toward the camp. One soldier recalled Black Hawk's voice that night as being "an almost unearthly sound." Later, his words were interpreted to mean "Friends, we fight no more." But, at the time, there were not Winnebagoes in the camp to interpret and Black Hawk's effort to surrender was for nought.

The tragic end to Black Hawk's attempted escape came twelve days later. The soldiers caught up with the fleeing Indians at Bad Axe on the banks of the Mississippi. As the Sauks tried to cross the river, the soldiers opened fire and slaughtered 950 of the tired and starving Sauks—men, women, children.

Black Hawk, however, lived. And later he would say:

"I would not have fought there, but to gain time for my women and children to cross to an island. A warrior will duly appreciate the embarassments I labored under—and whatever may be the sentiments of the white people in relations to this battle, my nation, though fallen, will award me the reputation of a great brave in conducting it."

final touches on his plan. It was for a city he called Madison, after James Madison, one of the nation's most popular founding fathers and a man known fondly as the "Father of the Constitution." Historian David Mollenhoff said the evidence points to Doty's selection of Madison's name being far from an accident but, instead, part of a wise and wily plan hatched by the former judge to assure selection of the Four Lakes site as the state's capital. In fact, Doty's deft maneuvering that fall in Belmont could well serve as a masterful blueprint for the army of lobbyists who have since lugged their briefcases up the steps of the state capitol. But then few lobbyists since have faced such a hard sell. There were eighteen other cities competing for the title, and Doty was pitching a site where no city existed, where boundaries were still marked by trees, and travel through the forests was by narrow Indian trail.

It helped, then, to offer a city named after Madison, who had died just five months before the legislators gathered in Belmont. Madison was the last of the signers of the Constitution to die, and

his death in 1836 had triggered a wave of sentimental feeling across the country. Doty did not stop there. He named all of the streets in his city after signers of the Constitution; the widest, grandest boulevard was named after Washington. Finally, Doty used a striking and familiar design for his city—a baroque radial street design with the streets radiating diagonally from an open and symmetrical square. It was, coincidentally or not, the same concept used by the architect

L'Enfant when he laid out Washington D.C.

It is unfair, probably, to ascribe all of Doty's motivation to opportunism. Doty, Mollenhoff points out, was a man who had seen the greatness of the Constitution at work in the courts of the still-new country. It is not unreasonable to think that he also wanted to honor the document and its authors with the city he was creating.

Still, Doty clearly knew what it took to play the political game. He was described in

those days as a man with a "handshake for everybody." And when legislators at the session complained of the cold and the chronic lack of firewood, it was Doty who quickly dispatched a man to nearby Dubuque. The fellow came rattling back in a wagon piled high with buffalo robes, which Doty promptly distributed to grateful legislators.

Then there was the mysterious matter of the corner lots. Mollenhoff noted in his history that between December 2 and 10, just a few days after the Madison site was approved, 16 of 39 legislators purchased lots in Madison—many of them choice corner lots—for prices ranging from 10¢ to $100 apiece. We will never know,

The northwest corner of Capitol Square in 1909 (top left), 1949 (top), and 1986 (above).

Another way to appreciate the city.

Mollenhoff says, whether the purchases were arranged before or after the vote.

For whatever reasons, late in the afternoon on November 23, 1836, members of the Senate, huddled in their buffalo robes, voted in favor of Madison as the site of the new capital. The House of Representatives followed suit on November 28. Thus, in appropriately political fashion, Madison came to be.

Of course, there was no Madison. Yet.

But if Doty was the first politician and lobbyist to lend his name to Madison's history, then a sturdy and enterprising couple named Eben and Rosaline Peck were the first entrepreneurs to understand the great business potential of the new and undeveloped state capital. Several Green Bay men who had attended the Belmont meeting stopped at the Pecks' tavern in Blue Mounds, west of the Four Lakes country, and told them of the decision to make Madison the capital. The Pecks, recognizing an opportunity, decided to open a public house on the isthmus; in April 1837 they left for the new capital in a wagon piled high with barrels of pork, flour, sugar, coffee, and the couple's ten-year-old son Victor. They made it that first day to Nakoma—today a posh neighborhood of large, shaded homes—where they camped for the night. In the morning they were awakened by the howling of wolves and an icy, windy spring storm that dumped six inches of snow on the ground.

The Pecks persevered, however, and Madison's first tavern and lodging place was open for business within days. Among their first customers, curiously, was a cranky English geologist named George W. Featherstonaugh. He called the area one of "the

Left: *State Assembly Chambers.*
Below: *The Capitol.*

35

Rosaline Peck, who was described by George W. Featherstonaugh as "a bustling little woman, about as high as the door…"

most exquisitely beautiful regions I have ever seen in any part of the world." He was less impressed, however, with the Pecks' modest establishment and left an amusing glimpse of life for the Pecks during those first rough and tumble days of settlement. He described the Pecks' combination lean-to/cabin as a "wretched contrivance," noted the low door (upon which he had conked his head), and the crowded interior of Madison's first hostelry stacked with crates and barrels and bags. He described Rosaline Peck as a "bustling little woman, about as high as the door, with an astounding high cap on."

The first capitol work crew, en route from Milwaukee, fared little better than the Pecks on their journey to Madison. It rained on the crew continually during their ten-day journey; the sun came out once, in a prairie ten miles northeast of Madison. They promptly named the place Sun Prairie, and another Dane County community (though nothing was there yet except the prairie) had a name. The 30-man crew arrived on the isthmus at 9 A.M. on Sunday, June 10, and celebrated by shouting and tossing their hats high in the air.

For long months, however, Madison remained little more than a clearing in the woods. The Pecks' humble inn became the community center for a while. Eventually a young fellow named Simeon Mills opened the first general store. A couple of taverns opened and, on one Sunday, Madison's first church service was held in one of the barrooms.

When, in November 1838, legislators convened for the first session in the nearly-completed state capitol, Madison consisted of about 30 frame and log buildings scattered almost randomly about a stump-covered hillside. The first meetings in the new tin-roofed capitol were, to say the least, inauspicious. The capitol itself, at least to some, was singularly unimpressive; one wag said it looked like a "toad crouched in the grass." Inside,

King Street looking toward the original capitol, from a watercolor by Johann B. Wengler, an Austrian traveling America. One wag said the structure looked like a "toad crouched in the grass."

it wasn't a very comfortable place at first. One of the legislators, Ebenezer Child, reported that when the lawmakers convened the green oak boards of the floors were frozen through and all the walls iced over. "Our ink would freeze," Child wrote. "Everything froze."

The basement of the capitol was full of pigs. Child, whenever somebody he disagreed with took the floor, put the hogs to good use. "When members of this ilk would be-come too tedious, I would take a long pole, go at the hogs, and stir them up," he wrote. "The speaker's voice would become completely drowned, and he would be compelled to stop, not, however, without giving his squealing disturbers a sample of his swearing ability."

Capital designation notwithstanding, Madison still seemed a wilderness outpost. There were no streets, just rough dirt pathways. Cows, chickens, and pigs roamed the capitol lawns during the day and at night on those same lawns Madison citizens hunted wolves, bear, and deer. Mosquitoes were horrible.

Prairie fires were a menace. In the lower reaches of the Isthmus, quicksand was a problem.

Still, within ten years Madison had graduated to a village, added sidewalks and built its first school. Pigs were still a problem; villages trustees hired a pig catcher. By 1842, the population had

CRAIG SCHREINER

Right: *The Keenan house, on Gilman Street.*
Below: *Paddle and Portage race.*

Facing page: *Olbrich Gardens.*

BRENT NICASTRO

grown to 172 residents. In 1848, Wisconsin became a state and the University of Wisconsin was established in Madison. January 1849 saw the arrival of the first telegraph message, and the Wisconsin State Historical Society was founded.

How did the city look then? In 1850 the isthmus was still so choked with trees and underbrush that one visitor called it "an inhabited forest." There were 1,672 residents. The first train arrived in 1854, and the streets were lighted by gas in 1855. Historian Mollenhoff suspects that sometime in the 1850s the residents of Madison endured their first traffic jam, probably on a fall Saturday when the streets were jammed with farmers trying to maneuver horses and wagons around the square.

By 1885, just a scant 40 years from the time when wolves roamed the capitol grounds, the square had become a major regional commercial center. There were 125 stores around the square—furniture and hardware stores, book dealers, restaurants, china stores, bakeries, drug stores, candy stores, saloons. Mollenhoff painted an enticing word picture of what it must have been like

then. Among the noises would have been the rumbling of streetcars with their flanged wheels, the clip-clop of horse hooves on gravel, the cries of newsboys hawking papers. Sewers were just coming into use, so the gutters downtown were still the main receptacles for slop from saloons and restaurants. Mixed with the horse manure, this was a

rather heady mixture to sniff while strolling about.

But there were good smells, too. The pungent odor of tobacco floated from tobacco shops, and the delicate fragrance of chocolate wafted from the candy stores. When the lawn on the capitol grounds was mowed, the smell was like a country pasture that had just been cut.

Pinckney Street in 1860.

Meat shops and groceries displayed beef and whole ducks and geese outside the stores. Tobacco juice was a nasty obstacle on the sidewalks.

By 1920, the square had undergone yet another transformation, thanks to Henry Ford. It looked not all that different than it does today and, certainly, many would recognize the early versions of Buicks, Chevrolets, Fords, Cadillacs, Dodges, and Oldsmobiles.

It was in the 1940s, however, that the square really came into its own. The big department stores had opened by then—Manchester's, Woolworth, Baron's, and J.C. Penney. It doesn't take a historian to recreate that time. There are many still around who remember the thrill of shopping and strolling the sidewalks then. In a 1987 newspaper interview, Bob Schmitz, who ran a clothing store that his family had opened years before, remembered the excitement of those years downtown, especially the Christmases.

"Oh, the Christmases!" Schmitz recalled. "People always said you hadn't seen Christmas until you'd been downtown, and it was snowing, and the trees were up on the street corners and Santa's house was up on the Capitol Square."

As the seasons changed in those days, so did the shopping atmosphere on the Square. One old-timer remembers that, almost on a given date in early spring, merchants would trade their wool suits and hats for spring-weight suits and straw boaters. Schmitz remembered how his father, Ed, would take straw hats and freeze them in blocks of ice and place the blocks in front of the store to monitor the coming of the warm weather.

Again, however, times changed. With the 1960s and 1970s came the growth of the city's suburbs and the arrival of the suburban shopping mall. Enormous malls grew on the city's east and west sides; downtown and the square lost some of its lustre.

But today it is on its way back. Empty stores are being replaced by offices and specialty retail shops, museums, bars and restaurant. Madison residents seem to have reclaimed the square in much the same spirit with which the city's founders carved the city from the wilderness years ago.

Today, for example, you can stroll on a Saturday morning around a farmer's market on the Square and buy fresh produce from the Dane County countryside—everything from morel mushrooms in the spring to fat squash and bright orange pumpkins in the fall. On every corner there are jugglers and mimes and crusaders for causes you didn't even know existed. There are stands selling gourmet coffee and fresh-squeezed lemonade. On Wednesday evenings in the summer, people come from miles around the city and county to spread their blankets on the sloping lawns, dine on lavish picnic dinners, and listen to the city's orchestra perform on the steps of the capitol.

And on one summer weekend always occurs an event that would seem strange indeed—or perhaps very familiar—to Madison's earliest residents. During a wild race called "Paddle and Portage," contestants paddle canoes up the shore of Lake Mendota to

East Washington Avenue in 1916.

the isthmus, carry their crafts atop their shoulders across the Capitol Square, and into Lake Monona where the race continues down the shoreline.

It is a remarkable thing to see dozens of overturned canoes being lugged up the steep sides of the isthmus and across the square. And more than one observer of the event has been known to stand watching and mutter, smiling: "Only in Madison! Only in Madison!"

41

The Workplace

The running joke about working in Madison is that there are more people with advanced college degrees selling shoes in the city than just about anywhere else in the country.

It is a comment not on the ability of the degree-holders but on the desirability of Madison as a place to live—no matter what kind of job you have to dredge up to stay.

The truth is, however, that there are plenty of very good jobs in Madison and Dane County. Both the county and the city have employment rates that always run several percentage points above the national average.

Where do people work?

Lots of people in the city work in the public sector—in government or university jobs. In fact, the University of Wisconsin and the state government are the two largest employers with 27,160 and 19,300 employees respectively. To get a clearer picture of these numbers, all you have to do is take a stroll on a summer day at lunchtime up State Street and around the Capitol Square. Both will be crowded with university and government workers on their breaks,

strolling and munching on food cart lunches and listening, perhaps, to one of the musical groups that invariably sets up during the noon hour on the capitol lawn.

Madison is also a big medical town. Both medical research and health care are important industries. The city is home to the University Medical School, five general hospitals, more than 20 major medical clinics and more than 100 research and testing labs. The UW-Hospitals & Clinics is one of the city's largest employers with 4,690 workers. The next two largest hospitals also rank among the city's largest workplaces; Meriter Hospital employs 2,850 while St. Mary's Hospital Medical Center has 1,900 employees.

Then there is Madison's corporate and manufacturing world. This interesting bit of history is worth exploring; it helps to explain the Madison workplace of today.

In the early 1900s, when the rest of the country was gripped by an industrial fervor and a fascination with manufacturing, Madison was engaged in a strange debate of the kind the city seems to still specialize in. This debate was between the city's business community and the city's more gentrified residents, its salaried university professors and government employees as well as the many doctors and lawyers the city had attracted. At issue was the future of industrial development in Madison. As explained by Madison historian David Mollenhoff, it was a doozy of a debate and its outcome helped shape the kind of economy the city enjoys today.

The business community argued for encouraging more heavy industry in Madison, going so far as to propose the construction of a municipal coal dock on Lake Monona so soft Illinois coal could be

brought up the Mississippi, Rock, and Yahara rivers and offered to factories that located in the city.

But the more genteel elements in the city argued against encouraging industrial growth. "This influential group," Mollenhoff wrote, "liked Madison the way it was—that is, as a sophisticated, quiet, clean, beautiful college town and state capital. They derived great pride from the fact that Madison had more persons listed in 'Who's Who' than Milwaukee had with ten times the population."

Anti-industrial forces feared most of all that factories would destroy the city's natural beauty. One writer, espousing this point of view, put it this way: "Reflect gentlemen, how many places there are which can be made big and how few places there are which God has made beautiful."

The surprising outcome of this debate was a compromise, reached after numerous confrontational debates at which everyone realized that neither side was all right or all wrong. Industrialists came to understand the drawbacks of heavy industry for a city of Madison's size and character—while their opponents came to the conclusion that the proper mix of industry and university, factory and government, was necessary to assure the city's economic health as well as cultural diversity. The result was a tacit agreement among the city's business and political leaders to encourage "high grade" factories employing highly skilled and highly paid workers. The factories would be located on the city's east side, at some distance from the university's tree-shaded grounds and quiet, hallowed halls.

The arrangement came to be known as the "Madison compromise," according to Mollenhoff. "The capital city," he wrote, "would have both factories and faculty, lunch buckets and brief cases, east side and west side. It was a comfortable world of cozy compartments separated by a socio-economic fault line that even today sends tremors through discussions of municipal problems."

But the compromise worked and it brought prosperity. The city's population increased by fifty percent between 1910 and 1920 and the number of factory workers increased by 283 percent.

Today, partly as a result of this history, Madison boasts more than the usual number of so-called "clean" industries. The insurance business, for example, is the third-largest employer in the city after the university and state government. Madison is the home base for several of the nation's leading insurance companies including American Family Insurance, CUNA Mutual Insurance Group, and General Casualty.

There are numerous other financial, professional, and technical service industries that call Madison home. At least three major corporations have

43

chosen Madison for their world headquarters—Rayovac Corporation, Ohmeda and Nicolet Instrument Corporation.

Rayovac is worth looking at a little closer. The company—a manufacturer of batteries for industrial and home use—has been in Madison since 1906. But by 1982, it had come upon hard times. The company had dropped to third in its market and was still dropping; it was losing $20 to $25 million a year.

Enter a guy named Tom Pyle.

Pyle, from New York, had gone to business school in Madison 25 years before. He was looking for a challenge. And he had very fond memories of Madison from his college days. Along with his wife, Judy, a marketing whiz who had served as marketing director for Elizabeth Arden and Estee Lauder, Pyle bought the faltering corporation. Six months later, they had completely redesigned the company's look and started the corporation back onto the road toward financial success. Much of their success was due to their own business savvy and a passionate attention to detail; it wasn't unusual to see

them on the production line making sure that the batteries faced front in their packages so the name would be easy for customers to spot.

But the Pyles credit of lot of the company's newfound success to Madison and to Ray-O-Vac's employees. Pyle, sitting in his office in the corporation's new Madison headquarters, said the kind of worker you'll find in Wisconsin and in Madison gives a distinct business advantage. There is a sturdy Midwestern work ethic and pride in the company's employees, he said. And it's a pleasure, he said, after having spent many years in New York, to come to work and find people smiling.

"People here just seem happier," Pyle said. "And there is an openness. People are friendlier."

Why the difference? Part of it, Pyle said, may simply be that Madison, especially compared to the country's bustling eastern seaboard, is a very pleasant, relatively stress-free place to live. Maybe workers here smile more, he said, simply because they don't have to worry about traffic jams on the way to and from their jobs.

There are dozens of other

long-established companies in the city that have come to understand and rely on the special qualities of Madison's workforce. All told, more than 25,000 people are employed in Madison-area manufacturing. Many of the companies have world-wide reputations. Who hasn't, for example, heard of Oscar Mayer, the giant food processor that made hot dogs famous? It's headquartered in Madison and is one of the city's largest employers, providing jobs for 2,700 people. And, yes, on pleasant summer days, the distinctive, hotdog-shaped Wienermobile still cruises Madison's neighborhoods offering free rides to happy kids.

Not all of the city's thriving businesses are giants, of course. In fact, the backbone of the city's economic base may still be the small business, the kind of Mom and Pop places that have long been a staple of America. The retail trade employs 41,200 people in the city, for example, and 53,900 people are employed in the service industry.

Consider, for instance, Markos Regassa. Every day over the lunch hour you'll find him manning his colorful food cart, selling spicy Ethiopian food on the university's Library Mall. His is a modest enterprise but Markos is an integral part of the city's business and cultural climate; in fact, Madison wouldn't be the same without him or the many other entrepreneurs who sell everything from food to flowers from wooden carts on the city's streets.

Markos is an Ethiopian expatriate who has made Madison his second home. He came to America and Madison in 1985 and in 1991 he graduated from the UW-Madison business school. For some time after his graduation, he worked three jobs, saving money to start his own business. Today, if you want to buy your lunch from Markos, be prepared to stand in line. His has become one of the city's most popular luncheon carts. The menu is unique in the city, featuring everything from dorwat, a hot Ethiopian chicken stew, to baris, Somalian curried rice with lentils.

Markos credits his success to hard work and to Madison's open-minded consumers. "In this business," he said, "quality and persistence are very important." His persistence has paid off. He's opened two new restaurants since he first backed his food cart onto the mall.

Finally, a survey of the Madison and Dane County workplace would not be complete without a look at the huge role that agriculture plays in the area's economic and cultural life.

Dane County is ranked among the top 10 counties in the nation in the value of farm products produced within its borders. These products include corn, alfalfa, tobacco, oats, eggs, cattle, and hogs, and every kind of dairy product imaginable. The county, according to the 1990 census, has 611,000 acres of farmland, 75 percent of the total acreage in the county. There are 3,010 farms in the county, with an average farm size of 203 acres.

Madison is fast becoming the center of the world dairy industry. Every year it hosts World Dairy Expo, a dizzying, dairying extravaganza that attracts experts in the field from around the world.

The city and the state are not shy about capitalizing on its dairy heritage. If you've watched the Green Bay Packers play on national television lately, you've no doubt noticed the huge plastic cheeseheads that invariably show up in the crowds.

And, living in Madison, you come to expect fertilizer advertisements on television and dairy promotions that will, somehow, always involve a big-eyed, black-and-white Holstein cow. Every summer, one of the most popular events on the Capitol Square is "Cows on the Concourse." It happens in June during one of the Saturday morning farmers' markets. Farmers bring their holsteins to town and line them up for everybody to see and admire. Yes, only in Madison.

But nowhere is the pivotal role of the farm economy more apparent than when you get into your car, leave the city, and head into the Dane County countryside. There, you'll find the red barns, the blue silos, the pastures full of fat cows, and all the land, spreading for miles. Roll down your window in the summer months and, more than likely, you'll smell the sweet aroma of fresh-cut hay. To the farmer, of course, it smells like a livelihood. To others, to the people who live in this good part of the country, it smells like home.

Institutions and Ideas

Picnic Point.

In February of 1849, when the first University of Wisconsin class convened, and the fledgling city of Madison was described by one wag as an "inhabited forest," the university staff consisted of one teacher, and the entire student enrollment numbered seventeen.

Relations with the townfolk were tenuous; the university was attacked in the press and by the local clergy for being nondenominational. Parents were warned to keep their sons away from the "godless associations of this atheistic institution."

Within the next couple of years, more students enrolled and North Hall, a dormitory and classroom building, was built atop wooded Bascom Hill overlooking Lake Mendota. Students divided their time between classes and hunting in the thick forests along the lake for game for their tables and wood to heat their rooms.

Life at the other end of State Street, where the tin dome of the newly built state capitol rose above the forests, was just as rustic. Legislators spent most of their time debating proposals to move the state capital elsewhere. There seemed no end among the pol-

iticians of complaints about the backwardness of the capital city—the streets that were always deep in either dust or mud, the clouds of mosquitoes, the pigs that ran loose in the streets. Madison residents, meanwhile, had their own problems with the politicians and their lifestyles. One newspaper editor harrumphed that "if Madison has more gambling dens, more grog shops, more houses of infamy in proportion to its population than most other cities in the state, it is because the people send representatives here who patronize and encourage such things."

From these humble and rocky beginnings, however, grew the two institutions that have done more than any others to shape the character of Madison. Residents in the city have always taken pride in being home to both the University of Wisconsin and the state capital. Visitors, certainly, have taken notice. No less a literary light than Horace Greeley, editor of the *New York Tribune,* wrote about the city's "magnificent" site after a visit in 1854 and told his readers how "the university crowns a beautiful eminence a mile west of the Capitol with a main street

Overlooking the west end of the University of Wisconsin.

connecting them à la Pennsylvania Avenue."

"Madison," Greeley concluded, "has a glorious career before her."

Today, Greeley's words sound prophetic indeed. The University of Wisconsin has grown into a world class institution of higher education

...it is also the students themselves; with their youth and their enthusiasm, they add imagination and humor to an already lively city.

with an enrollment of more than 40,000 students and a budget of $1.2 billion. Its graduate programs are ranked eighth in the nation and the university itself ranks fourth in the nation in research and development expenditures. One recent survey showed that forty-nine different undergraduate programs at the university rank among their respective top tens in the nation. There are twenty-eight general, professional, and special libraries across campus, with nearly 6 million volumes on the shelves. Twelve Nobel Prizes have been awared to UW–Madison faculty or alumni.

The university has become so much a part of the city that it is difficult to separate the two. University landmarks are Madison landmarks—Bascom Hill at the western end of State Street with its bronze statue of Abraham Lincoln, Library Mall with its food carts and its fountain and its clock tower, the Memorial Union Terrace with its view across Lake Mendota, and Picnic Point with its winding trails and its arbor-framed vistas of the Madison isthmus and the capitol dome. Just a few blocks from the 929-acre main campus is the University of Wisconsin Arboretum, a 1,276-acre natural preserve of pine and oak forests and restored prairies; it is one of the city's most striking landscapes, a dark and wild stretch of green where, from a snowy cross-country ski trail or from a canoe on gentle Lake Wingra, it seems impossible that you are in a city of nearly a quarter-million people.

On the city's far west side are still other reminders of the university's importance to the city. The 300-acre University Research Park is home to more than forty companies in fifteen buildings. Specializing in technology and research, the companies in the park are linked to the campus by a fiber-optic telecommunications network to provide easy interaction between the university and its own education and research programs.

The University of Wisconsin Hospital is another familiar Madison landmark, with its giant brick beehive of a building spreading above the city's near west side. The hospital and its medical school are the third-largest employer in Dane County after state government and the University of Wisconsin's Madison campus.

Madison wouldn't look the same if the University of Wisconsin were not here. Certainly the city wouldn't feel the same. Something changes in Madison when the students return to town. Part of it is the arrival of fall—perhaps the most beautiful time in the city—with the trees ablaze, the air crisp and clean, and the lakes at their bluest. But it is also the students themselves; with their youth and their enthusiasm, they add imagination and humor to an already lively city.

One winter morning a few

years ago, Madison residents awoke to find the "Statue of Liberty" buried up to her chest in the Lake Mendota ice behind the Memorial Union. An explanation came later in the day. The statue was the work of the Pail and Shovel Party, the daffy student political party then in control of student government. The party had won election by promising, among other things, to flood Camp Randall stadium and hold battleship races, and to move the Statue of Liberty to Madison. A party spokesman explained that the statue had been airlifted to the city but had come loose and fallen into the lake. The enormous replica drew thousands of people who trudged through the snow and ice to admire her plaster stare and upraised torch. The battleship races never materialized.

University traditions are nowhere more evident than on a fall Saturday when the Badgers play football in Camp Randall Stadium. The celebrating begins early in the day with tailgate parties in parking lots all across campus. Bratwurst sizzle on open-air grills behind the student union near the stadium. Beer flows and a Badger band plays polkas and "On, Wisconsin." The stadium itself nearly always fills, even during a lackluster season, and becomes an almost solid blanket of red by game time. Airplanes fly above the crowd towing advertising banners. In the stadium, Bucky Badger the mascot bounces, the marching band struts, and, at the end of half time, thousands of students and university alumni stand and slowly wave their arms back and forth during the emotional singing of "Varsity."

Traditions have always been a part of university life. Years ago, bonfires were an important part of any celebration, especially homecoming. The freshmen generally built the bonfire and another class connived to light the fire ahead of schedule. Perhaps the most famous attempt was by Charles A. Lindbergh, briefly a student at the University of Wisconsin, who climbed to the top of a tower in the old Red Gym building and fired incendiary rifle bullets into a pile of wood stacked by freshmen around the Historical Society flagpole. His attempt failed but, in a scene out of the movie *Animal House,* a group of sophomores in an armored car broke through the throng of defending freshmen and succeeded in torching the fire. The bonfire tradition fizzled out around World War II.

Yet another strange tradition, long since departed, was the annual bag rush in which freshmen and sophomore men fought for possession of sixteen straw-filled bags lined up in the middle of a watered-down and muddy campus mall. The practice died out in the mid-1920s when Madison citizens started complaining that the victorious students marching up and down State Street were indecently clad, a

The battleship races never materialized.

likely possibility because one object was to tear the clothing from the opposing team.

The University of Wisconsin has had a tremendous impact, also, on the wider world. Through the years, research at the university has led to hundreds of breakthrough discoveries in fields ranging from agriculture to medicine.

A few examples:
• In 1924, Professor Harry Steenbock discovered that when the skin of animals and

University of Wisconsin Badgers:
The team, the field…

...the band, the fan, the stands.

51

food surfaces are exposed to ultraviolet irradiation, vitamin D is produced and stored. It has since become common practice to enrich food with vitamin D by exposing it to ultraviolet light. The discovery helped to practically wipe out infantile rickets.

• In 1941, Harold Rusch,

Just as they would leave their mark on the earth, so their sojourn along the shores of Lake Mendota would mark them.

UW Medical School oncology professor, was the first to show which wavelength of ultraviolet light produces skin cancer.

• In 1957, Dr. Manucher Javid, UW Medical School professor of surgery, became the first neurosurgeon in the world to use a urea solution to alleviate the swelling in brain tissue that interferes with neurosurgery. The discovery revolutionized brain surgery.

• In 1970, biochemistry professor Har Gobind Khorana synthesized a gene. He

had been awarded the Nobel Prize two years before for his work in genetic coding.

• In 1987 Dr. Folkert Belzer dramatically improved organ preservation by using a cold-storage preservation solution. It was the first breakthrough in organ preservation in 20 years.

The university's influence can be traced, also, to the distinguished alumni and staff members who once sat in the classrooms and walked Bascom Hill. Just as they would leave their mark on the earth, so their sojourn along the shores of Lake Mendota would mark them.

Frank Lloyd Wright was a student here for a while. He lived in Madison with his parents as a boy and spent his summers on his uncle's farm near Spring Green. In the spring of 1885, Wright enrolled as a student at the university; he took only three courses over two terms. While he was a student, however, he also worked as a draftsman with Allan D. Conover, a university engineering professor who was supervising construction of Science Hall. Wright did some design work on the enormous red brick building and it stands today at the foot of Bascom Hill, one

of the first buildings the famous architect had a hand, however small, in designing. By early 1887, Wright had left Madison, bound for Chicago and fame. But he would return eventually to become the focus of the greatest and longest-running building controversy in the city's history.

The writer Zona Gale was a student at the University of Wisconsin from 1891 to 1901. She studied literature and penned sentimental poems and stories that appeared in *Aegis,* a campus literary publication. Later, after working as one of the first female newspaper reporters in Milwaukee and New York, she would write the novels—hard-edged studies in realism much different from her early work on the UW campus—that would gain her fame. In 1920, she published *Miss Lulu Bett,* a novel that shared honors that year with Sinclair Lewis's *Main Street* as the best selling novel of the year. A year later she was awarded the Pulitzer Prize for drama for her stage adaptation of the novel.

The naturalist John Muir, a father of the national park system and a founder of the Sierra Club, came to the University of Wisconsin from the family's frontier farm near

Portage in 1860. He attended classes for only two and one half years but later he would write that his studies at the university provided that "glimpse of the cosmos" that laid the foundation for his famous studies of the Sierras and glaciers and other mysteries of the natural world.

One of the nation's most noted historians—Frederick Jackson Turner—also rose to fame from a position as professor of history at the University of Wisconsin. Turner, who grew up in the small city of Portage north of Madison, turned the study of history in this country upside down in 1893 when he delivered his famous essay on the influence of the American frontier. Turner theorized that the continual push westward and the opening of newer and newer frontiers had shaped the American character—independent, ambitious, pragmatic, optimistic. Turner's thesis has been repeatedly challenged over the years but, despite its flaws, it remains a touchstone in the study of American history. Turner scholar William Cronon of the University of Wisconsin called this "the single most influential essay ever written by an American historian."

And, Aldo Leopold, the naturalist who almost single-handedly created the modern-day environmental movement, taught at the University of Wisconsin from 1933 until his death in 1948. Leopold developed the university's department of wildlife management, the first such in the nation. More importantly, drawing on observations from a lifetime in the field and from a run-down farm near Portage that he nursed back to health, Leopold developed his "land ethic," a new way of looking at a human responsibility for the land based on morality instead of profit. He outlined the prinicple in a wonderful book called *The Sand County Almanac.*

The accomplishments of these three men—Turner, Muir, and Leopold—have fundamentally changed the way we view the natural world around us. Cronon, in his essay "Landscape and Home: Environmental Traditions in Wisconsin," cites their "extraordinary efforts to discover a moral meaning for our lives upon the land." The work of all three men was greatly influenced by their associations with the University of Wisconsin and is testament, in turn, to the powerful role the uni-

versity has played in shaping modern thought and in making Madison a place known in the world's farthest corners.

From the other end of State Street has come an equally powerful influence on Madison's character.

Wisconsin's state government has changed considerably from the days when the basement of the state capitol was used to house pigs. In 1849, the year after Wisconsin became a state, the state government payroll included fourteen people. Today, full-time state government employees number more than 57,000, with another 12,000

Leopold developed the university's department of wildlife management, the first such in the nation.

serving in part-time jobs.

Wisconsin's state government achieved nationwide fame in the late 1800s and early 1900s as the seat of American progressivism under the leadership of Robert Marion LaFollette. During the course of his tenure as

ZANE WILLIAMS

ZANE WILLIAMS

Left and facing page:
On the University of
Wisconsin campus.
Below: *Madison
isthmus (Lake Mendota
on the left, Lake
Monona on the right).*

Wisconsin governor and as a U.S. Senator, LaFollette earned the nickname "Fighting Bob" for his fiery campaigns on behalf of political reform; he was set on his reformist course, supposedly, when a Milwaukee politician

Madison residents have always taken their politics seriously.

attempted to bribe him.

Some historians quibble with the extent of LaFollette's role in the progressive reforms that marked Wisconsin politics between 1900 and 1910. Still, the legislative agenda during those years was crowded with proposals that did everything from create a direct primary election to increase the taxation and regulation of railroads. The reforms continued when LaFollette left for the U.S. Senate and Francis McGovern became governor. From the legislative chambers atop Madison's isthmus came ideas that were unique in the country for their farsightedness and imagination: worker's compensation, a state income tax, a State Life Insurance Fund.

Just as State Street linked the University of Wisconsin and the state capitol in reality, the state's politicians during these years furthered an idea that linked the two institutions in deed also. The concept had been forwarded first by university officials a few years before—that the university and the state government work together to share the knowledge gained on campus with all the people of the state. It came to be known as the "Wisconsin Idea" and has become a cornerstone of Wisconsin political thought.

Whether it is due, perhaps, to such an illustrious political history or simply the nearness of the debate, Madison residents have always taken their politics seriously. It is everyone's hobby. As far back as 1917, a Madison newspaper writer noticed this city's preoccupation with all things political.

"In Wisconsin," the fellow wrote, "when two citizens meet, one instantly heaves a tough political argument at his neighbor, and the other responds by belaboring his friend with a wholly contrary idea. Then one of them mentions LaFollette, at which they grapple, pull hair, and roll over in the bushes. When

completely exhausted, they get up, shake hands, and go home feeling it has, indeed, been a profitable meeting, and that Wisconsin is the best of states to live in."

Perhaps because of the state's high political profile, Madison always seems to attract more than its share of campaigning presidential hopefuls every four years. Some of these appearances have been particularly memorable. Jesse Jackson gave a rousing speech on the capitol's State Street steps during his 1988 campaign. Bill Clinton and his running mate Al Gore spoke to a crowd of thousands on the south side of the capitol on a shining fall afternoon in 1992. It was a classic Madison political scene with high school bands, dozens of local politicians on parade, balloons and banners, and kids hanging from the branches of the trees on the capitol lawn. Clinton went on to win the state's presidential primary.

In the same way the city changes when the students come back in the fall, so does Madison change when the politicians arrive in town for the annual legislative session. When state flags are run up the flagpoles atop the south and west wings of the capitol, the Senate and Assembly are in session again and Madison becomes a political town.

During the long days of summer and during the breaks between sessions, the capitol rotunda echoes with the footfalls of a few tourists and the handful of street people who seek to rest for a while in the shadows cast by the marble pillars. But when a legislative session opens, the chamber doors are thrown open, the revolving doors at the capitol entrances spin like merry-go-rounds, and lights burn for long hours behind the frosted glass windows of legislative offices.

As much business, it seems, is done at the bar rails and at the tables of downtown eating and drinking establishments as in the capitol itself. On any given noon hour during a session, you can visit Kosta's, a popular Greek restaurant on State Street, or the cafes in the Concourse or the Inn on the Park and see men dressed suspiciously like politicians—or lobbyists—huddled in earnest conversation over food and drink.

Gus Paraskevoulakos, the garrulous owner of Kosta's, said there is a noticeable difference in his trade when the Legislature is in session. His place, with its roomy tables and plush chairs overlooking the bustle of State Street, has long been a favorite political hangout.

"If I recognize the politicians," Paraskevoulakos said, "I try to give them a nice secluded table, a nice corner where they can enjoy their meeting. Or lots of times they'll come in at lunchtime and they'll have pens and papers with them and they'll ask for a table so they can talk business and they'll stay until everybody else is gone and it's quiet and they'll talk, talk, talk, talk. They feel like it's home here."

Some nights downtown during a session are more memorable than others. Ironically, one of the liveliest nights in recent years at the local watering holes was the long night of debate over the proposed 21-year-old drinking age. The popular Signature Lounge at the Inn on the Park was nearly overflowing with people—legislators, tavern owners who had been bused in from all over the state, liquor lobbyists—and debate on the issue was to be heard at every hand.

Bill Plizka, a former Republican legislator from Mellen, remembered the night as the wildest of that session. The debate, he recalled, went on for more than forty hours at the capitol and there was a constant coming and going from various hangouts around the Square. Hospitality suites at the hotels were crowded the whole night with politicians and various lobbyists. Late in the debate, some legislators started switching their allegiances and tempers flared.

"It got real intense," Plizka said. "People were being lob-

> ## *"People were practically threatening to throw each other out the windows."*

bied very, very heavily. Over at one hospitality suite at the Inn on the Park there were some very heated moments. People were practically threatening to throw each other out the windows."

That's politics.

As Paraskevoulakos is fond of saying, "Life is a little better when the politicians are in town."

Right: Manchester Place reflects the capitol.
Below: Lake Mendota calm.

Facing page: Capitol decor.

ZANE WILLIAMS PHOTOS

An Architect's Legacy

A good idea dies hard. Especially in Madison. And especially when the idea is from Frank Lloyd Wright, the noted architect who was, for many years, one of Madison's most cantankerous and controversial characters.

Although it was long known as a city where ideas get debated nearly to death, Madison outdid itself deciding whether to build a dramatic Wright-designed terraced civic center on the downtown shore of Lake Monona. In the spring of 1993, Madison residents, after one last political squabble, finally approved building a convention center based on Wright's original design.

By the time the convention center is built, it will have been just shy of sixty years since Wright first unveiled the plan.

The delay was due to the city's penchant for political infighting and to Wright's often arrogant and abrasive style. Even though Wright grew up in Madison, built his home and established his architectural practice in nearby Spring Green, and remained in the Madison area from 1911 until his death in 1959, many of the city's residents never became comfortable

with the architect's flamboyant ways (he was often seen sweeping around town in a flowing cape, brandishing a cane) or his unconventional buildings.

Wright, from the very be-

A Wright design, the Jacobs house on Old Sauk Road.

ginning, was his own worst enemy in campaigning for approval of what came to be known as his Monona Terrace plan. When he first presented the idea, at a 1938 meeting of the Madison Lions Club, he

introduced himself as "Wisconsin's black sheep." He attacked the recently built state office building as a "monstrosity" and put down the state capitol as being "neither gentlemanly or scholarly." He then ripped Madison, calling it "a high-browed community of provincials" whose citizens were "lacking in civic spirit to build a new city-county building as it should be."

Wright offered redemption, of course, in the form of his own Monona Terrace plan, an architectural design he called a "great civic expression." Even Wright, accustomed to seeing his plans greeted with skepticism, could not have foreseen the controversy that lay ahead. Over the next fifty years his Monona Terrace designs would be shelved and revived a half dozen times and opposed, sometimes viciously, by council members, mayors, state legislators, governors, and others who would go so far as to enlist U.S. Sen. Joseph McCarthy, to attack Wright as being "un-American."

But Wright had his supporters, too. After all, during the course of his career, he designed 32 buildings for Madison, among them the now-famous Unitarian

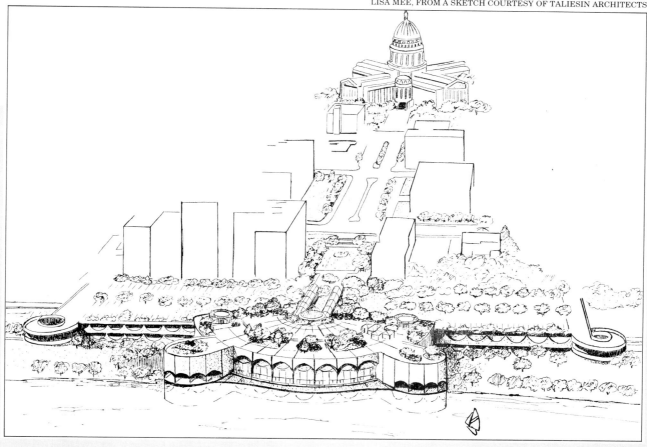

An early drawing of the Monona Terrace Convention Center, by a Taliesin architect.

Church and several private residences. And Wright's plans for Monona Terrace—a site he described as "the great chance at the foot of Monona"—were no less than visionary. Wright scholar Mary Jane Hamilton, in her essay "The Olin Terraces and Monona Terrace Projects," called the original design the most original of Wright's career that "must rank as one of the more inspired urban and civic gestures of all time."

Wright's original plan called would have housed government offices, a performing arts center, exhibit space, galleries, a jail, and even a rail-road station. It was a semi-circular, five-story platform that swept out over Lake Monona and echoed, in its design and in its glass, domed fountains set in lush gardens, the white dome of the state capitol at the opposite end of the street.

The updated design retains the basic appearance of Wright's original drawing and will include a 42,300-square-foot exhibit hall, a 15,000-square foot ballroom and banquet hall, a 1,000-seat multi-media auditorium, meeting rooms, and an enormous rooftop garden.

It is not exactly like Wright's original plan. Still, Taliesin Architects, the firm that Wright founded, has been hired to design the building and see it through construction and the plan remains faithful to the visions that the architect had for the site that so stirred his creativity.

Marshall Erdman, a Madison builder who worked with Wright and knew him well, laughed when asked what Wright would think about his plans for Monona Terrace finally becoming a reality.

"I know exactly what he'd say," Erdman said. "He'd say, 'It's about time you came to your senses!'"

Dane County

JEFF MILLER

Snowboarding competition at Tyrol Basin in Mount Horeb.

A good part of Madison's magic comes from the Dane County countryside around it, from the ease with which you can be gone, just like that, from pavements and tall buildings and into a gentle, timeless landscape of marsh or prairie or woodland.

There is plenty of varied country to wander around in. Dane County covers 1,205 square miles, from the wild-life-rich marshes and uplands along the Wisconsin River in the north, to the prairies and island-like burr oak stands in the east and the south, to the unglaciated hills and valleys in the west. Scattered across the land are farms—about 75 percent of the county is in farmland—with their red barns and blue silos and pastures browsed by black and white Holsteins, the cow of preference in Wisconsin.

As pleasant as the countryside are the villages. If Madison offers the perfect urban setting with its university and cultural life and bustling downtown, then these rural villages are the perfect reflection of that historic, pastoral America that used to be— Main Street and bandshells and one-chair barbershops and old men passing the day on benches outside hardware stores. All of these can still be glimpsed when you travel Dane County's backroads and sideroads. It is a fine county just to ramble in, to get lost in. I'll do a bit of verbal rambling in this chapter, taking you on a casual tour of the county, its landscapes and a few of its communities, from its wooded western hills to its eastern prairies.

When I first moved to Madison, I found myself drawn mostly to the Dane County countryside north and west of the city. I liked the up and down quality of the landscape in those places untouched by the glacier. At the far south-western corner of the county is the village of Blue Mounds. It is tucked into the base of the 1,100-foot hill from which the village takes its name. In the very early years, according to some histories, the hill and an adjacent, lesser slope were called the "Smoky Mountains" and, indeed, on some fall days and on those listless, steamy days in the dead of summer, the hills do seem wreathed by blue mists. They are prominent landmarks in the county and can be seen from 30 and 40 miles away. There is no better place to get a feel for the county's land forms than from the top of Blue Mounds.

A storm approaches the Mount Horeb area.

A pleasant state park there boasts trails and a campground and picnic areas and, on the very top, two viewing towers that pierce the sky like fire lookouts. From the tower on the western end, you can look west and see a folded, wooded landscape, or north toward the jungly banks of the Wisconsin River where it winds in its green, bluff-sided valley west to the Mississippi. From the eastern tower, looking toward Madison, you see a much different landscape, one tamed and gentled by the glacier 10,000 years ago and carved today into a mosaic of plowed and planted farmfields.

Below drowses the village of Blue Mounds. It is the earliest settlement in Dane County and, perhaps, the state. It owes its existence to the discovery of lead in 1828 by Ebenezer Brigham. Brigham had come to the area originally from near the mouth of the Missouri River. He had traveled first to Galena, the center of the excitement that was generated by the discovery of lead in the upper Mississippi country, and then to the Blue Mounds area where he discovered a valuable lead ore deposit. He settled in to work the deposit, building a cabin near a cold spring on the side of the

mound where he had a view of the prairie for miles.

Blue Mounds would become important, too, for its location on one of the earliest and most crucial overland travel routes in the state. This thoroughfare was along a series of high ridges that ran from the Mississippi to Madison and it became known as Blue Mounds Road or the Military Road because it connected forts in Prairie du Chien and Portage. J.R. Brigham, nephew of Ebenezer, recalled in an early history the four-horse coaches of the United States mail that used to travel the route, stopping at the public house in Blue Mounds. One of the showiest and most popular drivers was a fellow named Andrew Bishop, known by fellow drivers as "The Elder" because of his flair and experience. He later became sheriff of Dane County and then Madison's police chief.

A good part of Madison's magic comes from the Dane County countryside...

But, Brigham noted, neither post compared with the days when Bishop drove the great and rumbling stagecoaches, when he "lustily wound the sounding horn along the echoing sides of the Blue Mounds, and, with a cheery flourish of his long silver-mounted whip, brought his load of happy passengers up to the door of the house for dinner."

Today Blue Mounds is a quiet, sleepy place known mostly by those who pass through on the way to the state park. And the stagecoaches disappeared long ago, replaced today by bicycles; the famous old travel route through the town has become a popular cycling trail called the Military Ridge Trail.

Out in this part of the county, too, and just east of Blue Mounds on Highway 151 is the city of Mount Horeb, a popular tourist destination because of the city's rich Norwegian heritage and its numerous antique shops. Founded in 1850 and named for the Biblical mountain, Mount Horeb is a pleasant city with tree-shaded side streets and turreted Victorian homes. Wander around long enough and you'll come across what must be one of the world's only mustard museums, with mustards from all over the world and just about every state in the union. Also in downtown Mount Horeb is the Wisconsin Folk Museum with numerous exhibits of Wisconsin folk art and a gift shop. When you need a break, Schubert's, a homey restaurant on the main street, serves great pie and coffee.

In the countryside not far from Mount Horeb you'll find Little Norway, a pioneer Norwegian homestead. Nearby also is the Cave of the Mounds, a National Natural Landmark and one of the most significant caves in the upper Midwest. In the winter, the Tyrol Basin ski area is one of the more popular downhill ski hills in southern Wisconsin; it's perfect for families and, in recent years, has become especially popular among snowboarders, who are drawn by the hill's sculptured half-pipe snowboard run.

From Mount Horeb and Blue Mounds, you can drive north to the Wisconsin River through country that gives you a fine idea of just what the word "unglaciated" means. A lacy network of county roads runs through the hills and, with a good highway map, you can link any number of them up to reach Highway 14 and the villages of Black Earth and Mazomanie.

Black Earth, founded in 1850 and named for the excellent trout stream that flows through the middle of the village, is a busy farm town of about 1,100 people. The square tower of the Patron's Mercantile Cooperative feed mill rises in the middle of town and is visible for miles. As in many agricultural communities, the cooperative is part of the fabric of life in the village. You can buy gas for your car at the co-op's pumps, food for your cupboards at its grocery, clothes for your family at its general store. The co-op has been around since 1894 when it was founded by Norwegian farmers who traveled the countryside selling shares in the enterprise for $10 per share.

There is still a faint touch of wildness to this part of the county. It comes, maybe, from the rugged, boulder-strewn hills that refuse to be tamed by the farmer's plow or from the nearness of the Wisconsin River with its green and undeveloped flood plain. Sometimes, there are surprising reminders that, no matter the paved highways and the jets overhead, we are not all that far removed from the land and its wild tenants. I remember a hot and dusty mid-summer day when, working on a newspaper assignment about Black Earth, a photographer and I stopped at a farmhouse just outside the village and asked if we could hike to the top of a steep hill on the farm to take a photograph of the town below. A young farm girl, no older than nine or ten, answered our knock at the screen door. She agreed to show us a way up the side of the bluff. When we arrived at the top, the photographer realized he had forgotten a necessary lense. The girl said she would show me a quicker

way down the face of the bluff so down we went. About halfway down, the little girl stopped abruptly. She turned to me and said we should probably go the other way.

"Why?" I asked, anxious on the hot day to get back down.

"There's a snake up ahead," she replied.

"Oh, it'll move," I said confidently. "Let's go on."

"No, I don't think we should," she said, shaking her head.

Finally, I moved past her and glimpsed around the corner of a boulder into the path ahead. There in the sunlight on the dusty path lay coiled a fat timber rattler, a poisonous snake I knew inhabited these hills but had never seen.

"You know," I said to my knowledgeable guide, "I think we should go the other way."

I have walked very carefully in these hills and woods ever since.

It is just a few minutes from Black Earth to Mazomanie, a railroad town founded in 1843 by a group of English settlers and named for a Winnebago Indian, Man-ze-mon-e-ka, which meant "Iron Walker." There is an interesting small museum near the downtown, well kept by the Mazomanie Historical Society.

The village gives its name to one of the more curious natural phenomena in these parts. If you follow County Highway Y north out of town, you'll eventually come to the Wisconsin River flowing on your left and, on your right, a wooden sign marking the location of the Mazomanie Sand Barrens. Explore the area and you'll find yourself walking in a miniature desert, a land of gravel and sand created thousands of years ago as the Wisconsin River, swollen by glacial run-off, receded. There are the typical desert denizens like lizards and snakes. And there is even a species of prickly pear cactus that blossoms only in June for a single day.

But the star attraction up in this part of the county is the river. Farther north, above the dam at Prairie du Sac, the Wisconsin River has been thoroughly tamed. On one stretch there are 26 hydroelectric dams and 21 reservoirs. But down here, between Prairie du Sac and the Mississippi River, the Wisconsin flows free for 92 miles. Because the floodplain of the river is so wide and wild—tangled backwaters, steep bluffs, shifting sandbars—there has been almost no development along its

Right: *Colorful Mount Horeb snowbirds.*
Below: *Near Black Earth.*

Facing page: *The Wisconsin River.*

shores. The river is likely to remain wild, too, because of state legislation passed in the 1980s. Now known as the Lower Wisconsin State Riverway, the lower 92 miles of the river are protected from development. It was a necessary and foresightful step, because the river is within five driving hours of about 15 million people in four states.

There are few better rivers on which to launch a canoe. In fact, what was to become Dane County was probably first glimpsed by Europeans who floated by in canoes. More than likely, it was Father Jacques Marquette and Louis Jolliet, the French explorers credited with first paddling the Wisconsin and discovering the Mississippi in 1673.

Not long after I moved to Wisconsin, a friend and I paddled the length of the Lower Wisconsin from Prairie du Sac down to the Mississippi. I was shocked by the wildness of the river and its valley. In four days we saw only a handful of people. Our days passed in languid fashion, liquid as the water on which we floated. We camped on sunwarmed sandbars, ate fat catfish that we caught in the deep and fast-moving channels, and let the river carry

us during the long days. Around each bend would be another vista more beautiful than the last—the broad and silver river, the green and distant islands, the blue bluffs in the far distances descending one after the other down to the river. At dusk, V-winged nighthawks filled the sky above the still riverwaters, swooping and soaring in search of insects. And at night the river bottoms were another world, a strange and dark paradise that made us think of Marquette and Jolliet crouched before their fire, listening to the booming hoots of the great horned owls coming from far back in the forest shadows.

It was a grand, eye-opening trip. I am reminded of it whenever I draw near the river.

This part of the river, near Mazomanie, reminds me also of a writer named August Derleth. He lived and worked just across the river in the Sauk County village of Sauk City and left us an eloquent chronicle of life in a river town, a record of village street lights flickering on in the summer evenings, of distant train whistles, of whippoorwills calling from the hills. It was his custom many evenings to walk across the rail-

road trestle below the village and into a thicket of sloughs and riverbottom woodlands on the Dane County side of the river.

"The tracks," Derleth wrote in *Walden West,* "led through lowland areas for some miles, east of the Wisconsin, lowland that was a rewarding diversity of woods, sloughs, meadows, and marshland, where great fields of Joe-Pye weed shone lavender in late summer and autumn, meadows flamned green in spring, oak groves vied with willows and osiers...

"In this haven of birds and frogs and lesser beasts I walked the evenings away, year on year, except when mosquitoes plagued me too much or the cold became too intense. I walked the cinderpungent railbed through the evensong of birds and the primitive cries of the batrachian population of this lowland and found there not only surcease from the day's tribulations but often also resolution of creative problems and balm for the oppressing irritations of existence common to all men."

The railroad track is still there, curving through the bottoms, and I've walked it many times, always finding the same peace sought by Derleth.

There is another interesting stop to make before leaving this northwestern corner of Dane County. It is, of all things, a winery. As you drive along Highway 188 on the Wisconsin's southern bank, it is somewhat of a surprise to come across the carefully tended grapes climbing up the steeply-tilted fields toward the ridgetop. They are part of the Wollersheim Winery.

The winery was started in 1847 by a Hungarian count named Agoston Haraszthy. Foiled by Wisconsin's severe winters, he relocated to California where he founded that state's very successful wine industry. But the fields he left behind in Dane County remained planted in grapes over the years and today, thanks to sturdier French hybrid vines, are the foundation for a thriving and popular winery. At the wine festival on the first weekend in October, if you are of a mind to, you can roll up your pants cuffs, climb into a wooden barrel, and stomp grapes.

Driving east across northern Dane County you pass into the rolling prairie lands, as beautiful in their own way as the western hills and valleys. Visible in this part of the county, too, are the sprawling suburbs with their big homes and cul-de-sacs. They've sprouted fast as the weeds that used to grow in the former farm fields around communities like Waunakee and DeForest and Cottage Grove. All these rural serve

Our days passed in languid fashion, liquid as the water on which we floated.

today as bedroom communities to a growing Madison and are struggling to retain some of their own identity.

Dick Emerson, publisher of the DeForest *Times-Tribune* and a native of the community, talked about the phenomenon with a Madison newspaper reporter. DeForest, according to the article in the *Wisconsin State Journal,* saw 481 people move to town in the 20 months between April 1990 and January 1992, a burst equaling nearly 10 percent in the village's population. Most of the newcomers work in Madison.

"If you go down Main Street or Holum Street between 6:30 and 7:30 in the morning, it's the grand exodus out of town," Emerson said. "Then about from 4:30 to 6 at night, it's everyone coming home."

Still, there are things about the village that keep it a small town. There is, for example, Pat Syverud, DeForest's Welcome Wagon hostess who, you can bet, met every single one of those 481 new residents mentioned above. The irrepressible Syverud said she meets an average of 20 new families a month and leaves with each one a basket filled with everything from civic information to free products from local merchants. These newcomers may come for jobs in Madison, she said, but they live in DeForest because it is a small town with all of the good things American small towns have always been known for.

"People will bring you to the window and show you the view," she said. "That's what they like: the trees, the view, the feeling that they're away from it all."

Once, many years ago, this entire area was an immense prairie. It's hard today to imagine the size and the feel of it. Not far from DeForest,

From the skies over Sun Prairie. LARRY MAYER PHOTO

though, there is a place that can give you an idea of what the country around here used to be like. Owned and maintained by the Madison Audubon Society, it's called Goose Pond Sanctuary and it's just across the Columbia County line a few miles north of De-Forest. Here you'll find dozens of acres of restored native prairie. The pond itself is modest enough but its waters and its surrounding marshlands have been a stopover for migrating

birds since long before man ever came to the area. It is still one of the prime locations in the county for seeing hundreds of species of waterfowl. Sue and Mark Martin, caretakers of the sanctuary for many years, keep careful track of the comings and goings of the various species. By their count, as many as 27 species of waterfowl, including rare birds like white-fronted geese and European wigeons, stop to rest at the pond during migration.

The pond's popularity as a rest stop—for birds and humans—can be explained by its history. In the 1830s, when the first settlers came to this part of the country, Goose Pond was surrounded by 60 square miles of prairie, rolling hills covered by Indian grass and big bluestem that grew as high as a horse and moved in the wind like a rippling sea. It was a beautiful land bound only by sky and distant horizons. And in the middle was the blue of Goose Pond.

Hugh Jamieson, one of the earliest settlers, wrote in 1851 about the pond where there was water to slake the thirst of travelers on the prairie: "It was a tiresome journey to travel over the prairie in those days. Not even a drop of water was to be found except at a small pond called the Goose Pond near the center or about half the distance across."

Travel back south into Dane County, down Highway 51 and then east a ways on Highway 19, and you'll come to a small city that takes its name from the prairie. Sun Prairie received its name on June 5, 1837. On that day a group of 45 workmen passed through the area on their way

Left: *Syttende Mai festival at Stoughton.*
Below: *Yahara River near McFarland.*
Bottom: *Sun Prairie.*

71

from Milwaukee to Madison, where they were to begin work building the new state capitol. It had been a miserable trip; the travelers had endured nine straight days of drenching rainfall. But as they passed this spot on the prairie, a bright and drying sun came out to warm them. So happy were the workers that one of them immediately carved the name "Sun Prairie" into a tree to commemorate the moment.

Today, Sun Prairie's great-

It was a beautiful land bound only by sky and distant horizons. And in the middle was the blue of Goose Pond.

est claim to fame may very well be a groundhog—Jimmy the Groundhog, to be more exact. Jimmy, every year, vies with Pennsylvania's Punxsutawney Phil to provide a reliable prediction concerning the end of winter—a much sought-after prediction in this place where winter often seems to linger through midsummer.

Sun Prairie is also the host of one of the county's most popular small-town festivals. Every summer, soon after the local sweet corn ripens and is at its peak of freshness and sweetness, the city hosts the Sun Prairie Sweet Corn Festival. Tons of sweet corn, boiled and dipped in vats of melted butter (real butter, of course—it is Wisconsin) are served up to thousands of hungry visitors.

South of Sun Prairie is Stoughton, another Dane County city with a rich Norwegian heritage. Every summer the city holds a rousing Syttende Mai festival that attracts huge crowds and includes a popular but rigorous marathon run from Madison up and down many hills to Stoughton.

Stoughton is also famous for the beautiful Norwegian art of rosemaling, the colorful painting of delicate and intricate flowers on everything from plates to wooden shoes. Per Lynse, an artist who specialized in rosemaling, emigrated from Norway and settled in Stoughton in 1907. He had been well trained by his father who had taught him all the traditional rosemaling designs. Lynse continued the tradition and is credited with reviving the unique art form in the United States in the 1930s and 1940s.

East of Stoughton, perched on the Dane-Jefferson County line, is the picturesque village of Cambridge. Its quaint downtown is home to a thriving pottery industry that attracts bus tours throughout the year. There are two main stops—Rockdale Union Stoneware and Rowe Pottery Works, both on Main Street.

Cambridge has another claim to fame. Back in the early 1900s a farm boy named Ole Evinrude was on a lake outing with his girlfriend, picnicking on an island. His girlfriend decided she wanted ice cream so Evinrude hopped in the rowboat and rowed to shore. On the way back, a strong wind came up; Evinrude rowed harder, the wind blew, the ice cream melted. It was time, Evinrude decided, that somebody invent a motorized boat. So he did. By April 1907, Evinrude had perfected his invention and demonstrated it to a wide-eyed crowd, cruising by the audience at a whopping five miles per hour. He went on to form a corporation to build the outboard motor; the company still exists today as the Outboard Marine Corporation.

Driving west across the

bottom of Dane County, headed back again toward the unglaciated hills, you'll come across a number of tobacco fields. Tobacco is one of the state's little-known agricultural products. Some Wisconsin farmers tried as long ago as 1844 to grow tobacco, but did not meet with much success. A couple of farmers named Ralph Pomery and J.R. Heistand tried again in 1853 and grew an excellent crop. Tobacco, especially in the Stoughton area and further south around Edgerton in Rock County, has grown into an important crop. You'll see many of the long and rectangular drying barns in southeastern Dane County. Today, 90 percent of the domestic cigar wrappers come from Wisconsin.

Almost directly south of Stoughton is one of the area's most historically significant villages. Just across the county line in Rock County is Cooksville, founded in the mid-1800s. Today, the entire village has been declared a National Historic Site and there are 22 buildings listed or eligible for listing in the National Registry of Historic Buildings. Many of the homes in the community have been restored. You can't drive

through town without a stop at the Cooksville General Store; it's a classic, mainly because rather than being a touristy attraction it's a working general store where farmers come to get tobacco planting supplies and area mothers bring in their babies to get weighed on the store's big produce scale.

Continue east and you'll come to Belleville, a Dane County village with maybe the strangest story of all to tell.

The village of about 1,500 is a pretty place on the Sugar River with a park-like town square and a tidy main street. But it wasn't until 1987 that it started gaining attention— as a place favored by UFOs. In March of 1987, the area around Belleville became the focus of nationwide attention as more than a dozen UFO sightings were reported, including one by the village's police officer.

Experts were called in and were baffled when they discovered that the objects were also being picked up by a radar tracking station operated by the Federal Aviation Administration in Aurora, Ill. The experts eliminated every possibility—conventional air traffic, weather balloons, stars, planets and military aircraft.

The strangest story of all

came from a fellow named Harvey Funseth, a surveyor for the state Department of Transportation. Driving home from work one evening between 5 and 5:30 P.M. Harvey saw four oblong objects in a formation in the sky. He drove to within an eighth of a mile of the objects and watched as one dropped out of the formation. It moved silently across the sky leaving a vapor tail in its wake. It had no wings and no tail and had a flashing light on top.

So there you have it. A quick tour of a strange and beautiful county...

Harvey grabbed a camera that he had with him and snapped seven pictures of the object. Later that week he picked up the processed film. Those seven frames were blank. The rest of the photos on the roll were fine.

So there you have it. A quick tour of a strange and beautiful county called Dane. From mist-shrouded hills to deserts and rattlesnakes to wild rivers to Norwegian art to UFOs. What more could a person want?

The People

Winter Carnival "ice divers" on Lake Mendota.

You cannot know a city or a landscape until you know the people who have made it their home. It has been my good fortune over the years to be a newspaper reporter on the city streets and on the rural backroads, poking around in every corner of Madison and Dane County, searching out other lives.

I have become acquainted with all manner of people who call this place theirs; I've spent time with them and listened to their histories and their troubles and their dreams. And I've written their stories. The wealthy and the homeless. Newly-arrived immigrants and lifelong residents. Farmers and auto mechanics. Corporate executives and professors. Plumbers and politicians. Architects and school crossing guards. Black and white and American Indian and Hmong and Korean and Chinese and on and on.

There is magic in this rich mix. For its size and its location in the northern Midwest, Madison is remarkably diverse and cosmopolitan. A good part of this sophistication comes from the University of Wisconsin with a world-class curriculum and faculty that attract students, teachers, and researchers from around the globe. The university ranks fourth in the nation for foreign-student enrollment, according to the Institute of International Education. This diversity is readily apparent on and near campus. A stroll along Library Mall on campus and down State Street toward the state capitol is as revealing of this country's wonderful cultural mix as any walk in New York or Boston. A look at the restaurants alone is enlightening. Here in this city of 200,000 you can eat food from Thailand, France, China, Nepal, Africa, India, Korea, and a dozen other places around the globe. Or you can, of course, stick with traditional Wisconsin—bratwurst and beer.

Consider, as further evidence, this story told by Mary Carpenter, manager of the farmer's market, about an unusual meeting at the popular Saturday morning market.

"One day," Carpenter said, "a graduate student from Israel was purchasing lamb, and another customer came to buy lamb as well; he turned out to be a grad student from an Arab country. The two started trading recipes on the spot. Maybe that's a better system of getting them to-

BRENT NICASTRO

Left: Art Fair on Capitol Square.
Below: Tenney Park.

ZANE WILLIAMS

75

gether than [formal] negotiations."

Madison, from very early on, has always attracted a diverse and intriguing population. It's amusing to note that the first celebration of Independence Day on the site of Madison was recorded in 1836, and it was eight French fur traders who did the celebrating. In 1848, the population of the wild and wooded isthmus and new capital was

There is magic in this rich mix.

mostly Yankee, native-born settlers who hailed from the country's Eastern Seaboard. But by 1856, a scant eight years later, more than half of the city's residents were foreign born. They came, mostly, from Germany and from the Scandinavian countries. Today, the city's residents are from all over the world, and the fastest growing segment of the population is from Asia.

But to really get a feel for the people themselves, you have to go beyond such generalities. You have to get out and talk to people, meet them in the places they work and

live, hear their voices, see their faces, listen to their tales. For this chapter, I interviewed several people who live and work in Madison, people who have thought about living in this place. They are all different—a newspaper columnist, an architect, a taxi driver, a social worker, a businesswoman, a minister. But they are also alike because Madison and Dane County is their home. Some of them were born and grew up here. Others moved here and never left. All of them are bound by the same sense of place and belonging; here they have found something that speaks to them and is important to them, be it a job that connects them to the city, a niche in the thriving business community, kinship with family and friends, or an affection for the gentle, beautiful landscape.

When Steve Hopkins talks about Madison and about the rural Dane County countryside in which he grew up, the city and the landscape come alive. He has been on intimate terms with this part of the world all his life. On dusky summer evenings he goes to fish the same cow pasture creeks he fished as a boy. They are the same creeks his

father fished, the same creeks where Hopkins taught his own son Peter to fish.

His past ties him to this place. He's thought a lot about it over the years and he's written about it, too, as a columnist for the *Wisconsin State Journal* in Madison. Over the past 30 years he has developed a loyal following, readers who have come to know and respect his deft and subtle renderings of the southern Wisconsin countryside and of its people and of the small and large episodes of his own life. Running through his writing, always, is an alertness to the natural world and to the powerful role it plays in all our lives. Hopkins seems most at home in the outdoors and is most often seen in chinos and faded work shirts, even at his office desk. His favorite escape is a jaunt to the unglaciated hills of southwestern Wisconsin where he has a cabin that he built years ago in the wooded cleft between two steep hillsides. At his Madison home you'll find three canoes clustered around the woodpile and a jointed flyrod leaning against the fireplace.

He is comfortable, too, in the small towns and in the main street cafes and in the rural taverns where you can still get a tap beer for a quarter and where you can catch up on local gossip. We met one cold spring day for Manhattans and hamburgers in the dim and comfortable interior of a popular Madison tavern. We perched on our bar stools and talked about writers and writing, about fishing, about canoeing, and about the good country so close at hand. One of the things Hopkins likes best about living in Madison is that you are never far from a trailhead or a creek.

"I like Madison," Hopkins said, "because it's a city with city conveniences and because it has almost everything you'd want in a much larger city. But, unlike a lot of other, larger cities, there is almost a rural aspect to Madison. From anywhere, you can be out of town and into the country in a matter of minutes."

Hopkins, now a youthful-looking sexagenarian, grew up in the western Dane County village of Mount Horeb. It's a small farm town in the unglaciated hills that mark the rest of southwestern Wisconsin. Hopkins' father, Walter, was a barber and some of Steve's earliest, fondest memories are of his father's barber shop with its stove and big barber's chair and the easy, friendly banter that was always to be found there.

"My early education," Hopkins once wrote, "was gleaned from the conversations of men waiting their turns for shaves and haircuts—the shopkeepers, the livestock dealer, the Lutheran minister and the Catholic priest, the feed dealer, the lumberman, the doctor, the dentist, and the farmers."

Most of his youth, it seemed, was spent outdoors. Mount Horeb is surrounded by hills and valleys and there are clear trout streams flowing through many of the valleys and there are lakes full of bass and panfish scattered about. Hopkins loved to fish for suckers on Mount Vernon Creek, a beautiful narrow trout stream not far from town where redwing blackbirds still chatter at fishermen, and the water gathers after fast, shallow runs, in slick, black pools beneath overhanging birches and cedars.

Hopkins has never strayed far from his hometown. He served a stint in the Air Force repairing sea rescue planes in the wilds of Alaska. But he returned after his tour and moved to Madison, twenty miles from Mount Horeb, where he went to the University of Wisconsin and, eventually, went to work writing for the *Wisconsin State Journal*. He married and raised three

All of them are bound by the same sense of place and belonging...

children in a comfortable ranch home on the city's west side. It has been a fine place to live and to raise a family, he says now, looking back. The family spent its vacations outdoors, canoeing and fishing Wisconsin waters in the summer and skiing its hills in the winter. Their house is a happy clutter of outdoor gear and books and dogs and cats. Hopkins has captured all of this life in his columns, the child-rearing and the trips and the country.

"It's nice country, good country," Hopkins said. "Outdoor writers do their best work when they write about good country that they know and like. I write best when I write about Dane County and about Madison."

In recent years, Hopkins has found himself looking

CRAIG SCHREINER

Steve Hopkins

even closer at the landscape he has spent his life in. He has developed an interest in the geology and the archaeology of the area and has tramped the hills and the lakeshores with geologists trying to learn how the place got to look this way.

"Much of Madison is on terminal moraines and drumlins," Hopkins said," and the lakes are the products of glaciers. I like knowing that I'm sitting on what a glacier probably piled up. I like knowing that sandhill cranes have been around here for fifty million years and that it will be forty million more years before man even approaches that. I feel like a very temporary resident here. We all are."

Knowing the land so intimately has only deepened Hopkins' respect for this corner of the world. He travels widely in other places; his home is filled with wildlife prints from his Alaska journeys and with rugs and artwork from his many trips to the southwestern deserts. But Madison and Dane County will always remain the places he comes back to.

"It's a good place to have your roots in," Hopkins reflected. "A person has a more satisfying and fulfilling life if you live in a place that you like and you have a sense of that place and you have ties to the land…You have all kinds of places you like to travel in. But in your heart there is only one place that you call home."

If Hopkins derives his sense of this Wisconsin place from the countryside, then Bruce Algozin finds his on Madison's city streets. At night. Behind the wheel of a taxi cab, a red and white 1984 Dodge Diplomat with no shocks and too many thousands of miles on its odometer to matter anymore.

I joined Algozin in his taxi late on a Saturday night midway through his 3 P.M. to 3 A.M. shift. It was a mild

evening and the doors of the downtown bars stood open to let in the cooling air. The sounds of the city after dark floated out and over the sidewalks and the streets—the backbeat rhythms of the jukebox, the clink of glasses and the click of pool balls and the murmur and the laughter of the night's citizens.

Wallace Stegner and other writers who have explored the importance of place in our lives say knowing about our human presence on the landscape is as crucial to understanding place and belonging as knowing about the glaciers and the mountains and valleys they left behind. Stegner, in his essay "The Sense of Place," commented that writer Wendell Berry gave a very human dimension to his definition of place. Berry, Stegner writes, says that "knowledge of place comes from working in it in all weathers, making a living from it, suffering from its catastrophes, loving its mornings or evenings or hot noons, valuing it for the profound investment of labor and feeling that you…have put into it."

"He is talking," wrote Stegner, "about the knowing that poets specialize in."

Algozin, driving through the city night in his taxi, is as

Above: Bruce Algozin.
Top: Another sign of Madison's diversity.

much poet as hack. He is, in fact, a writer when he isn't driving. But there is much poetry, too, in the work that he does, in the way he celebrates the people of the city and in the skillfull, accomplished way he gets them where they want to go.

The city becomes a different and more lyrical place from behind the wheel of Algozin's

He remembers the life that was in the books and, in contrast, he remembers feeling the constraint and the isolation of the classroom.

taxi. In Madison taxi jargon, the dark stretch of Regent Street between two sections of a near west side cemetery is called the "bone zone." The International House of Pancakes far out on the west side's Odana Road is called the "O-HOP." The same pancake house on University Avenue near campus is called the "U-HOP." Madison General Hospital has been shortened to

"Gin." When Algozin calls the dispatcher from the intersection of Fish Hatchery Road and the Beltline Highway, he is at "Fish and the Belt."

The dispatcher on that night was a fellow nicknamed "Curly." Among the other drivers on the streets during my night's ride were "Da," and "Snoozy," and "Mean Gene." Algozin is called "Boomtown" because of a newsletter called "The Boomtown Rat" he published a few years ago during a labor dispute.

Algozin has been driving either part- or full-time since the early 1970s. He came to Madison as a student from California in 1967 at the height of the anti-war protests that marked those years, and he can remember sitting in his apartment on Dayton Street and feeling the sting in his eyes from the teargas that floated through the streets. He stayed through those tumultuous years and stayed and stayed and stayed. His is a story that can be heard repeated many times in Madison—that of the college student who came for the University of Wisconsin but got drawn deeper and deeper into the city and its life and eventually, almost without realizing it, went native.

But Algozin's love for Madison as a place, as a home, didn't really begin until after he left the classroom and slipped for the first time behind the wheel of his taxi. He remembers taking an American literature class and reading the works of Hemingway and Faulkner and Steinbeck. He remembers the life that was in the books and, in contrast, he remembers feeling the constraint and the isolation of the classroom. About that time, he started driving a taxi. It was a revelation.

"There was something about it," he remembers, "that was just so honest. It was so real…I liked it. I liked the contact with real people. These people I was meeting in the street, they were grappling with real problems."

Whatever the reason, Algozin found more inspiration and more life on the city's streets than in the classroom. He also found a home.

"Once I started driving a cab, once I got out into Madison, that was the first time I really started feeling like it was my town, like I belonged here in some sense. I mean, as a student, you come and you go. You don't have any roots."

That was more than fifteen

years ago. Algozin married in the meantime and he raised a family. But he has never given up on the streets and on the people who clamber into the back of his taxi in the night.

As he drove, Algozin was like a tour guide to a city that hums and shakes and moves to an urban rhythm. He cruised the city, talking and listening, always listening, to the sing-song voice of the dispatcher reporting the location of fares. Algozin knows the city like he knows the rooms and hallways of his own house. He knows where he is, always, and knows what combination of streets, alleys, and shortcuts through parking lots will get him quickly where he wants to go. With the old car bouncing in and out of alleys and swaying around corners, he kept up a running commentary on the places he knows. The cavelike spot beneath an overpass on campus where kids sing rap until 3 A.M. on weekends. The stretch of the causeway across Lake Monona where the view of the city is most striking. He loves showing off the city.

"What's fun is to bring somebody in from the airport," he said, driving the causeway, the city glowing like Oz in the night sky ahead. "People are amazed when they see the city. And you get to live the first time you saw the city all over again."

The people keep Algozin behind the wheel of the cab. He loves the thrill of it, the edginess of it, the feeling that you never know who might be climbing into the taxi at your next stop. "You see maybe fifty or sixty people a night," he said, "and it's always stranger than you expected."

But the thing that is so striking about Algozin is the obvious affection he has for all of these people. They are the people of the city and he accepts them, wonders about them, cares for them; the young and weary black woman at the bus station with the beautiful child, the happy young couple who share a cigarette in the back seat and talk about their plans for the evening, the two Hispanic men going home from their jobs in the kitchen of a west side restaraunt.

There was a call around 1:30 A.M. from the Ideal Bar on the city's east side. We pulled up in front of the bar where the door was propped open and we could hear the deep bass of the jukebox inside and see the dark forms, wreathed in smoke, around the bar. Algozin shined the taxi's spotlight through the tavern's wide plateglass window. "Honking the horn," he

"...you get to live the first time you saw the city all over again."

said, "isn't very effective because of the jukeboxes."

Out of the bar came a woman in her late teens or early twenties. As she walked to the car, Algozin said he knows her, has been hauling her on Saturday nights between her house and the Ideal for years. She got in and Algozin said her address and the young woman nodded and smiled. She was quiet the entire time. Algozin drove, watching the city going by his window, listening to the dispatcher. The tires thumped on the pavement. The urban night, in all its life and color, swirled by the windows.

On the far east side of town, at the very edge of a tract of small ranch homes that are clustered next to a dark and open field, Algozin wheeled the taxi over to the curb. The woman handed her fare across the seat, thanked Algozin for the ride as she was getting out, then walked toward the back gate of one of the homes. The neighborhood is dark and isolated. Algozin straightened the bills, watched the woman walk toward the house. When she was safely inside the door, Algozin pulled back into the night.

Linda Callif, a 29-year-old social worker, finds her Madison in the basement of the beautiful old Grace Episcopal Church on the Capitol Square. There, at a drop-in shelter, she helps tend to the needs of the city's homeless.

It might seem a depressing job upon first glance. But Callif is tirelessly cheerful. She helps manage Transitional Housing, Inc., the nonprofit corporation that runs the shelter and ten homes around the city that are used to house the homeless as they seek to make the transition from the streets to a more settled life. She is a familiar and encouraging figure to many of the city's down-and-out, savvy enough in the ways of the social work maze to figure out how to solve even the knottiest of their problems and see to just about any of their needs.

Linda Callif with a client.

She took time out one spring morning after the shelter had emptied of its guests from the night before to talk about her job and about the city that has become her adopted home. She is a sincere and intense woman with dark black hair and sharp, intelligent features. The enthusiasm she feels for her work and for Madison are apparent in her voice and in the way her words tumbled out as she answered questions.

"When I'm talking about Madison with friends, I brag a lot," Callif said. "The beautiful lakes, the farmer's market, the fact that it's a small city but doesn't feel like a small city...I love this place."

Callif's is the familiar story of the college student who

Left: *Alex Gee.*
Below: *Something for everyone on Lake Monona.*

came to the University of Wisconsin to study but stayed after earning her degree. She has lived in other cities, including Milwaukee and San Francisco. But Madison, she said, is a unique and special place. It has to do, she said, with how the city looks and with the character of the people who live here. This last thing she started to see soon after she began working for Transitional Housing in the mid-1980s. Madison, at that time, was beginning to change, to grow. There were more poor in the city, more people on the streets in need of shelter. But Madison re-

It has to do...with how the city looks and with the character of the people who live here.

sponded in a way that impressed Callif deeply.

The homeless shelter was opened and volunteers suddenly showed up by the hundreds. Today, she said, the shelter could not operate were it not for the 1,500 volunteers who come on their own—or representing any of fifty orga-

nizations, from churches to the telephone company, whose members and employees have organized volunteer groups. They come from all walks of life. They are bankers and parole officers and doctors and housewives. They work at the shelter serving food, passing out blankets. Restaurants from across the city provide food; businesses provide supplies like toothbrushes and blankets and clothing. A dry cleaning business cleans all donated clothing free of charge.

"We have volunteers who are very poor themselves," Callif said. "They bake cookies and that kind of thing. I know they don't have a lot themselves. But they want to help."

Even the city's young people are involved. Callif told of a group of high school students who decided to hold a fund raiser for the shelter. She expected a bake sale or some other modest effort. Instead, she said, the students staged a professional-caliber show and raised thousands of dollars. And they made a point of coming to the shelter and meeting the people who stayed there and learning about their problems.

What makes Madison different? The people in the city,

Callif said, have an attitude. When they see something not right, they want to correct it. "It's an attitude of wanting to make this a friendly, healthy, happy, and safe city for others," she said.

In Madison, Callif said, people refuse to accept that others are hungry or going without clothing. "In Madison," she said, "you don't see slums. People don't accept them. And it's not the government. It's the people themselves."

When she's not at the shelter, Callif is often outside. She spends hours walking and biking the city.

"I love working downtown," she said. "I love walking down State Street and watching people. You can pop into a million different bookstores; each has its own little specialized market. There are lots of coffee shops and flowers shops. And there's all the greenery and the capitol. In the summertime, there's always something going on. There's usually somebody out hawking their political views. The other day I passed McDonald's and there were people picketing hamburgers and encouraging them to serve veggie burgers. One morning I was downtown and there

Right: *Janice Durand.*
Below: *Life on State Street.*

Facing page, top: *Racing through Capitol Square.*
Bottom: *Longenecker Gardens, University of Wisconsin arboretum.*

CRAIG SCHREINER PHOTOS

87

Park Bank. I went to Lincoln School. And I went to the University of Wisconsin. I liked knowing the people I went to college with were friends I went through third grade with. I like knowing that my baby will have the same pediatrician I did."

It's this sense of community and belonging that Gee hopes to instill in the kids he's working with through the Nehemiah Corporation. The youth have a wide range of problems. They have been truant, have commited crimes like armed robbery, have been the victims of abuse at the hands of alco-

She has felt something in the air and on the streets and in the old and beautiful buildings.

holic parents. The Nehemiah Corporation, Gee explained, matches mentors with these young people, adults or young adults who spend time with them, taking them to movies, helping with their homework, or just talking.

"Already," Gee said, "we're finding that children who wouldn't talk to their teachers or their parents or their foster parents are talking to their mentors. We're showing them love. We're befriending them. We're not afraid to use the 'L' word."

Another arm of the organization is working directly with families, teaching parents how to be better parents, intervening via counseling and support when things threaten to fall apart.

"We're trying to teach people to take control of their own lives," Gee said.

Gee, who works seven days a week, often ten hours a day, has been so pleased with the Nehemiah Corporation that he allows himself to dream about the future. He envisions a school, an African American educational center, a program to help African Americans start their own businesses, a program to provide housing.

"I want to see people have hope," Gee said. "I want to see them enjoy life."

Janice Durand, one of Madison's most creative and successful merchants, has her office on the upper end of State Street in the heart of downtown. From her window she looks out over rooftops and parking lots and the rising brick walls of the city.

This is Durand's place. This busy urban setting is where she belongs. Thin and sharp-featured and intense, Durand seems to draw her energy from the concrete and the noise and the people shoulder to shoulder on the State Street sidewalks below. As practical and as down to earth as she is, Durand takes on all the characteristics of an old-time evangelist when she starts talking about downtown Madison and the role it has played in her life and in her success as a businesswoman.

Years ago, a bored and listless housewife looking for a way to change her life, Durand staked her future to downtown Madison. From her earliest days in the city she has sensed something special about downtown. She has felt something in the air and on the streets and in the old and beautiful buildings. She believed in downtown in the days when others looked at State Street and especially the Capitol Square and saw a place bypassed by time, eclipsed by the shopping malls. Back in the mid-1980s, when things looked most bleak, she was singing the praises of central Madison.

"The identity of the city is right down here," she said in one newspaper article. "Call it the psyche, the soul."

Durand grew up in Chippewa Falls in north-central Wisconsin and first lived in Madison when she was in her twenties and just married. She and her husband lived for a while in the Phillipines working in the Peace Corps and returned to Madison the same month John F. Kennedy was killed in Dallas. Ironically their return to Madison had been inspired by Kennedy's call for the nation's young people to do something for their country. Madison, they knew, was a place where it was easy to become involved, where politics seemed to be everybody's business.

"We came here to be political," Durand said. "It's a political city."

But Durand's true love affair with the city would not really flower until 1978 when, divorced and looking for something to give her life again, she turned to the place that made her feel most alive—downtown Madison. First, she wrote a Madison guidebook called *Getting the Most Out of Madison.* It sprang, she said, "out of my love for the city." She worked for a while in the gift shop of the Elvehjem Art Museum on the University of Wisconsin campus. And then she was hired as the first director of the newly-built pedestrian mall around the Capitol Square and up and down State Street. It was a perfect job, considering her passion for the place. She had hundreds of ideas for events and promotions and threw herself into the job. She came up with the idea for what became one of the most popular farmer's market events of each summer—"Cows on the Concourse," a dairy promotion that features as its centerpiece live cows on the Capitol Square for the kids to see close up and touch.

The job taught Durand a valuable lesson—the people of Madison loved the downtown as much as she did. There was a ready and willing audience for any number of events, as well as customers for a variety of specialty shops. She saw how much people loved to stroll the downtown streets, to nose around inside the striking capitol, to sprawl on the thick grass beneath the trees on the capitol lawn, to enjoy a meal or a cup of coffee at a quaint streetside cafe, to browse inside the book stores and the gift shops.

"I really think the best thing about Madison is its human-sized center," Durand said. "It's so easy to find the heart of the city here, literally and figuratively. You come down here on a Saturday and you're in the middle of it. And it's so manageable in size. You can cover it all by walking."

Although Durand loved the

"I really think the best thing about Madison is its human-sized center."

job, she burned out within less than a year. She let her enthusiasm get the better of her and became involved in everything; she even put up Christmas trees at the corners of the Square and, when they didn't look just right, trimmed them herself.

"I was driven," Durand remembers.

Durand finally left the job but turned to what seemed to have been her real calling and the thing she had been unknowingly preparing herself for. Durand had noticed that a storefront in a quaint old building on upper State

Right: *August in Madison.*
Below: *Marshall Erdman.*

Facing page: *Along Lake Monona.*

LARRY MAYER

91

Street was for sale and, the more she thought about it, the more it made sense. Owning a specialty gift shop on State would keep her downtown, keep her in touch with the interesting people who frequented the area, and satisfy her need to do something challenging and creative.

Durand had learned that people associated downtown Madison with specialty shops

"I don't ever see leaving here. This is my place."

and, on recent trips to other cities like New Orleans, she had noticed the popularity of small toy stores offering unique items.

Operating almost entirely on intuition, Durand opened a toy store in 1979. It was a different kind of toy store, filled with interesting and quirky playthings for kids and adults—kites and jigsaw puzzles and games and dinosaur toys. She called her store "The Puzzlebox" and counted on the curiosity and imagination of Madison's downtown shoppers to help her succeed.

"I had learned that the downtown market was very

innovative," Durand said. "They're the ones who like to try things first…It's a question maybe of values; these people are well educated and well read and they're just willing to try new things."

The store was wildly successful. Within months it had become as much an institution and as much a required stop for downtown visitors and their kids as the library and the capitol rotunda. What's more, Durand's odd and fascinating little store opened the way for dozens of other specialty shops, restaurants, and bookstores that, over the last fifteen years, have brought people and prosperity back to downtown Madison.

Durand went on to open toy stores in other cities including Milwaukee and St. Louis. Recently, anxious for further challenges, she sold the stores and moved on to a different kind of retailing. Just a few doors down from the original Puzzlebox, she has opened yet another specialty gift store called "Little Luxuries." It appears headed for the same success as her toy stores.

Looking back on the risks she took and the success she has enjoyed, Durand feels that Madison—its special

qualities of tolerance and innovation—had much to do with her rise in the local business community.

"I guess I found Madison far more empowering than any other city I'd been in," Durand said. "Nobody ever told me here that I couldn't do anything that I ever wanted to do. I never felt anything ever held me back…In 1985, I was looking to open a fourth toy store and I went looking for another city. But I never found one with the exact qualities of Madison. This is where I want to be. I don't ever see leaving here. This is my place."

If you ask Marshall Erdman what Madison means to him, what his sense of this place is, he'll take you back to a time when he was young and building homes, when he was befriended by a man the world knew as an odd and quirky genius, and he'll tell you how he came to build one of the city's most beautiful and beloved churches.

Erdman, now successful and wealthy beyond any of his early imaginings, will tell you that what happened to him in this city is like something out of a dream.

An interview with Erdman

takes a while. He owns and operates a building company with offices across the country and known around the world for its prefabricated buildings and its specialty now—medical buildings. During an interview at the company's headquarters on the city's west side, he sat behind a huge desk in the cluttered corner of an office that is filled with art—modern paintings and sculptures and an ancient stone Buddha. The phone rang constantly. It was usually business, although during the interview he also took time out to handle some civic duties and to arrange a vacation with friends in Arizona where, he enthusiastically told one caller, the desert flowers were more beautiful than ever before because of recent rains. He laughed often and although he was nearing seventy, his face retained the boyishness that is so apparent down through the years in the yellowing newspaper photographs.

As Erdman told the story of his past, he slowly drifted away from the present and the ringing phones and became caught up again in the bustling Madison of the 1940s and 1950s; he was a young immi-grant from Lithuania (he still retains a touch of the lilting accent), just beginning his career, and anything seemed possible in the city with the gleaming capitol and the university by the blue lake.

Erdman first came to Madison in 1942. He had come to America as an exchange student and was enrolled at the University of Illinois, where he had been studying architecture on a scholarship. He came to the University of Wisconsin campus to visit a friend who had been jilted. Although his friend's love affair was irreparable, Erdman himself fell in love—with Madison. He still remembers the lakes and the beautiful campus, and the Memorial Union with its dark and inviting Rathskeller.

"There was even beer being served in the union!" Erdman recalled with a laugh. "It was a different world."

There was something else that Erdman felt in Madison. Not far away, in a low wood and stone home that seemed to grow along the brow of a hill near Spring Green, the architect Frank Lloyd Wright lived. Wright's life, even by then, had become mythic and young architects around the world understood the strange-ness and power and importance of his work.

"Frank Lloyd Wright was close," Erdman remembered thinking during that first visit to Madison. "You always

...what happened to him in this city is like something out of a dream.

had that in mind."

It wasn't until after World War II, however, that Erdman would move to the city that would become his home. During the war he served as an engineer in France and Germany, where he helped build the famous Remagen pontoon bridge which allowed General George S. Patton's tanks to cross the Rhine and roll into Germany. Upon Erdman's return, he came to Madison and the University of Wisconsin. Still feeling the impact of the war, he enrolled to study foreign relations with the idea of entering foreign service after graduation. But the challenge and allure of building buildings was too much to resist and he returned to his study of architecture.

93

Right: *The Nutcracker at the Civic Center.*
Bottom right: *Near Verona.*
Below: *Hockey, anyone?*

Facing page, top: *Capitol Square holiday parade.*
Bottom: *Snowboard slalom competition at Tyrol Basin.*

Not long after settling in Madison, Erdman married. And one of his first building projects was an apartment to live in with his new wife, Joyce. Housing was at a premium and Erdman remembered prowling the city looking for something close to campus. He found a big prairie-style home on Carroll Street and noticed that the basement was unfinished. He offered to remodel the basement into an apartment if the owner of the home would then rent the apartment to him. The deal was agreed upon and Erdman enrolled in vocational school so he could use the school's tools to remodel the apartment.

Erdman eventually started building a few modest homes along Midvale Boulevard on Madison's west side. Then, in 1948, came the moment that Erdman has always considered the most important, the most telling of his career. Everything he would do afterward, he said, grew from it.

In 1946, Frank Lloyd Wright agreed to design a new church for the First Unitarian Society. The old church on the square had been purchased by Manchester's Department store and was to be demolished to make room for a parking lot. A deal was struck with Wright to build a new church on University Bay Drive in Shorewood Hills. Wright told the congregation he could build the church for $75,000.

Wright's design was stunning—a fieldstone marvel that spread low along the site and then rose above its chapel in an expanse of glass and stone and copper folded together like praying hands. But bids, Erdman recalls, came in much higher than the $75,000 Wright and the congregation had agreed upon. By fortunate coincidence, Erdman had built homes for some members of the Unitarian congregation. Building-committee members met with Wright and suggested Erdman as the builder. At first Wright refused, telling the members he did not want to work with an amateur.

But as the bids continued to come in much higher than expected, Wright relented. Erdman was summoned to Taliesin, Wright's Spring Green home.

"To me," Erdman remembered, "it was like going to see Saint Peter."

Erdman arrived at 1 P.M., the time designated for his appointment. But Wright was taking a nap. Erdman didn't dare protest. Instead, "I cooled my heels," he recalled. Finally Wright appeared, wearing his sweeping cape and brandishing an elegant cane.

"He looked at me," Erdman recalled, "and he said, 'Baby, how would you like to become famous?' Those were my introductory words from Mr. Wright."

Erdman, of course, agreed to build the church. How could he not? He was to be paid a $5,000 fee (which he never received).

There started, then, a period of Erdman's early career that he'll never forget. Building what has become one of the country's most famous churches was the thing that launched his career. But it also almost ruined him.

"It made me," Erdman said, "but I have never gone through more agony."

In the late summer of 1949, work started on the church. It was like few other construction projects the city had ever seen. Members of the congregation, Erdman said, hauled the stone for the new church from a quarry thirty miles away in Prairie du Sac. They hauled the stone in Erdman's truck and in their own trucks and cars.

The stillness of Tenney Park.

They worked every weekend for months, and Erdman was amazed. They hauled fifty tons of rock the first weekend; by May 1950, they had hauled a thousand tons. Those who couldn't help haul stone served refreshments or helped begin weaving a giant Wright-designed partition for the church's interior.

Despite such hard work and dedication, progress was slow and money always short. Finally, with the outside of the church nearly done but the interior still skeletal, money ran out. Wright summoned Erdman. Wright, Erdman said, was furious that Erdman had not finished the church within the budget.

"He told me how disappointed he was," Erdman said. "I started to cry, I was so hurt."

Erdman was so stricken he took drastic action; he hocked his life insurance and his mortgage to help raise the $6,000 that was necessary to plaster the walls and ceiling. "It was the best money I ever spent," he said.

The church was finished. Wright was happy; he never mentioned his tongue-lashing of Erdman again. In fact, the two collaborated on many projects, including a series of prefabricated homes that brought Erdman even more attention across the country.

Erdman went on to a successful and immensely satisfying career. He opened offices in seven other locations around the country. He was befriended by Madison's finest over the years, by governors and senators and mayors. For a time, he lived in Switzerland.

But Madison, the scene of his first and one of his greatest successes, has always remained his home. "I always tell people," he said from his University Avenue office, "that I don't know where else I'd live."

The Future

These, of course, are the problems of modern-day America. Increasingly, our success and our future as citizens on this globe become tethered less to the material benefits of growth and development than to the way we treat each other and the way we tend the earth beneath us.

On clear summer afternoons, when the sailboats are like so many billowing pennants on Lake Mendota, Madison seems as perfect a place as there is on earth.

But Madison does not exist apart from a changing nation, a changing world.

In recent years change has come to Madison, too. Much of the change stems from the increasing number of people living in the city and the county. Lots of people want to live here. Between 1980 and 1992, the population of the Madison urban area grew from 218,000 to 244,000. Growth has brought a more diverse population and increasing social and cultural awareness. Continued growth has also given Madison a measure of prosperity unusual during a time when other cities of similar size have struggled. Here, housing starts have continued to climb and property values have increased. New businesses have continued to open their doors. And the unemployment figure in Madison and Dane County is nearly always considerably lower than those of state and national averages.

Still, growth has exacted its price.

Madison and Dane County's burgeoning population has brought all the puzzles and dilemmas that growth anywhere brings. There is a familiar list now of social problems—increasing crime, more drug use, the appearance of gangs on city streets and in the neighborhoods, racial tension. Since 1980, the number of poor people has increased from 24,000 to more than 32,000. Violent crime has exploded by more than 80 percent and juvenile violence has risen more than 90 percent.

The environment has also suffered as more and more people move to the area. The farmland and woodland that has so shaped the county's character through the years is disappearing at an alarming rate. Every year, 4,000 acres is chewed up by development. It is replaced by subdivisions and strip malls and parking lots. Dane County Executive Richard Phelps calls this a "terrible loss" that is changing the very character of the county and the city.

"It would be terrible," Phelps said, "if we became just neighborhood after neighborhood. The beauty here now is of a more fragile, subtle type. And we will ruin it."

There is more than appearance at stake. With so many people, the pressure to build is so great that houses and subdivisions are going up where they shouldn't, on land that is too steep, in wetlands, or over springs that recharge the fresh water supply. Phelps points out that there were once twenty-three springs around Lake Mendota; only nine are left today.

"You put development in an area," Phelps says, "and that dries up the groundwater. You build wells for subdivisions, you lose the fresh water going into the lakes."

There are other environmental threats. When builders put up homes and apartments and parking lots on hillsides, it creates more runoff—often tainted by pollutants—and the runoff ends up in the city's four lakes. More silt is dumped into the lakes, too, and the lakes fill in and begin do die much sooner than they would naturally. Lake weeds are a growing problem because of this increasing silt load.

The city's air suffers as much as the landscape and the lakes. More people bring more cars and more air pollution. And anyone who drives the Beltline Highway to work and back can tell you that Madison now has full-fledged rush hours.

These, of course, are the problems of modern-day America. Increasingly, our success and our future as citizens on this globe become tethered less to the material benefits of growth and development than to the way we treat each other and the way we tend the earth beneath us.

But Madison, with its share of problems, has more than its share of solutions. It's a city given to ideas. It's always been so. And it's not surprising to discover that the solutions being discussed by policy makers in Madison and in Dane County rely heavily on the senses of place and belonging people feel here, and the senses of commitment and moral obligation that the sense of belonging creates.

It's not a new idea. In fact, it is the very thing Aldo Leopold was talking about when he first wrote of his "land ethic" in *The Sand County Almanac.*

"In short," Leopold wrote, "a land ethic changes the role of *Homo sapiens* from conqueror of the land-community to plain member and citizen of it. It implies respect for his fellow-members, and also respect for the community as such."

Richard Phelps learned early about this special closeness people feel for the landscape they call home. He grew up in hilly southwestern Wisconsin and developed a deep fondness for this countryside. As county executive, he hoped to touch that same sense in others to guide Dane County toward public policies that protect the county's unique environment. If you feel you belong somewhere, Phelps said, then you are more likely to want to protect that place.

"It's a feeling," Phelps con-

But Madison, with its share of problems, has more than its share of solutions.

tinued, "of knowing where you belong, of being in a place that captures who you are…This keeps you from feeling that your surroundings are disposable. And you do things that reflect long-term concerns."

In Dane County, Phelps said, this special attachment to the landscape is apparent and it translates into strong support for programs that use tax dollars to heal or prevent further harm to the environ-

Above: Richard Phelps.
Right: Paul Soglin.

Above: *A vital feature of Dane County.* ZANE WILLIAMS PHOTO
Left: *Fall yield.* BRENT NICASTRO PHOTO

101

ment that is so important to residents.

Phelps cited, for example, a conservation fund that was created by Dane County. The fund purchases environmentally sensitive lands to protect them from development and to help create buffers between villages and Madison's suburbs.

"...the rules that we decide, as a community, will govern our life in this place."

Dane County dollars, Phelps said, have also helped clean up the county's watersheds and improve land use so that less runoff and fewer pollutants are being dumped into the Madison lakes. One of the state's premier trout streams, Black Earth Creek, has also been restored to health with county tax dollars.

"We're seeing an increasing amount of tax dollars go into a long-term agenda," Phelps said. "People have accepted that. That's encouraging."

In the city, as well as in the county, the senses of place and belonging and community that link the people who live here hold out the promise of providing answers to the difficult problems of the future. Few people have thought about this more than Madison Mayor Paul Soglin. Although he is from Chicago and came to Madison as a University of Wisconsin student in the 1960s, Soglin long ago became a Madison native at heart. At this writing he was in his third term as mayor and was raising a family here—something, he says, that has added immeasurably to his sense of this place being a home. He's seen Madison through some of its most controversial years and has already left his mark on the urban landscape in the form of the State Street Mall, the Civic Center, and the soon-to-be-built Monona Terrace Convention Center—all projects he helped shepherd through the city's intricate political maze. He's a man who takes his job and his obligation to the community seriously; in 1992, driving the city's Beltline Highway, he took it upon himself to help police nab a couple of speeders. And, while in the hospital for angioplasty in 1993, Soglin took the news of the city's first murder of the year very personally.

"I see that as a violation of community standards," Soglin told a Madison reporter. "I see that as an affront to the entire community because we're trying to create an environment in which people express themselves in ways that are not violent."

Like Phelps, Soglin believes that the strong attachment people feel to this place, this city, can be used to bring peace and order and safety to a Madison that is beginning to suffer some of the same urban terrors of larger cities. It can be done, he said, through community standards—the rules that we decide, as a community, will govern our life in this place.

"Long before there were written constitutions or bills of rights or affirmative action programs or smoking ordinances, there were community standards," Soglin said. "Community standards have to do with how we relate to one another. Do we envy and respect drug dealers? Or do we teach our children alternatives to violence. Do we place a high value on education?"

Madison has always set its standards high, Soglin said, and often judges itself too harshly.

"We engage in a lot of self-criticism. We're not as liberal as we'd like to be. We're not as open-minded. We're sheltered. But when all is said and done, we've really done a very good job. Something has to account for the fact that, after all these years, we're still one of the best places in the country to live and raise children."

Indeed, in 1993, Madison was named in a nationwide survey as the top city in the nation in the country for raising kids.

Part of Madison's success can be traced to its history, Soglin said, and to the forward-looking policies initiated during the Progressive era. But Soglin also gave much of the credit to those private citizens in the city who give time and energy and money to make Madison a good place to live. Over the years, he said, the city has been fortunate to have politicians, religious leaders, newspaper publishers, and ordinary citizens who have made it their business to speak out about social problems and who have taken it upon themselves to make Madison better, to clearly state and live by the community's high standards.

It continues. Consider, for instance, the story of Vera Court, a cluster of twenty deteriorating apartment buildings on the city's northeast side. They provide important and hard-to-find housing for low-income residents. But the apartments, built in the 1960s, are showing the years. Mailboxes have been kicked in and doorbells are broken. Security doors are inoperable, hallways are dark, and carpets are threadbare. Dianne Rucks, who moved into a Vera Court apartment with her family in 1991, was unable to get her air conditioner repaired, or get her apartment's flimsy and unsafe front door replaced. She worries about her kids.

In other cities, especially larger cities like Chicago or New York, Rucks and the other residents in the apartments might have simply been forgotten in the press of other urban crises. But in Madison, a group of civic leaders banded together to buy half of the Vera Court apartments and remodel them. The group is called the Future Madison Housing Fund; it's an offshoot of the Greater Madison Chamber of Commerce and was formed after chamber members toured Vera Court and other low-income neighborhoods in Madison. Impressed with how hard Vera Court residents were working to improve their neighborhood, the members decided to spend $450,000 to remodel 64 apartments and install new carpeting, appliances, lighting, and energy-efficient furnaces. The group also planned to lower the rent for each two-bedroom apartment from $425 a month to $400 a month.

"What's exciting to me about this," Soglin says, "is

"Something has to account for the fact that, after all these years, we're still one of the best places in the country to live and raise children."

that they did it on their own. These are people who are taking on financial and social risks. The easy thing to do would have been to sit where you are in your offices and write out a few checks. But these people are out there.

"We're setting standards in the community where people actively participate, where community leaders are aggressively talking about the social compact, talking about how we relate to one another...There is a difference here."

Above: *Bascom Hill, up State Street, and to the capitol.* BRUCE FRITZ PHOTO
Top: *The capitol rotunda in holiday dress.* ZANE WILLIAMS PHOTO

104

Above: *Vernacular brick architecture enhanced for the Fourth of July.*
Top: *Lake Wingra wetlands.*
Left: *The Ace brothers on their farm.*

105

Epilogue

There has always been a difference here. This has always seemed a different, better place. The difference is in the way it looks and feels here, in the distant and beautiful views of the city's lakes from the tree-shaded lawn of the State Capitol, in the quiet of a pine woods deep in the Arboretum, in the gentle wildness of a cattail marsh on the edge of town.

The difference is in the way people live and think here. The differences are to be found in a taxi driver who watches his charges safely into their homes, a mayor who chases speeders, a geologist who divines the past of the place from messages etched in stone and sand, a group of students who relocate the Statue of Liberty to the ice of Lake Mendota, a businesswoman who feels the city's heartbeat in its downtown streets, a black minister who can see the city's future in the eyes of the kids he helps set upright again after they tumble. These are among the poets who are helping to sing the city into the future.

The magic they have sensed and that they pass along comes from long ago, from the earliest days thousands of years ago when the Paleo-Indians made their camps on the high land above the marshes, from the summer night in 1828 when the lead miner Ebeneezer Brigham made his camp in a clearing on the still-wild isthmus, looked out on "the strange beauty of the place," and predicted the growth of a city.

The city is here. The landscape continues to enchant. And its citizens, still under the spell of the lakes and the hills and the countryside and the city they have built, continue to invest their hearts in this place they have made their home.

For Further Reading

Bletzinger, Andrea and Ann
Short, editors. *Wisconsin
Women: A Gifted Heritage.*
The American Association of
University Women, Wisconsin
State Division, 1982.

Cronon, William. *Landscape and
Home: Environmental Traditions in Wisconsin.* The State
Historical Society of Wisconsin, 1991.

Draper, Lyman Copeland. *Col-
lections of the State Historical
Society of Wisconsin.* State
Historical Society of Wisconsin, 1909.

Gard, Robert E. *University Madison U.S.A.* Wisconsin House
Ltd., 1970.

Hove, Arthur. *The University of
Wisconsin: A Pictorial History.*
The University of Wisconsin
Press, 1991.

*The Lee Papers: A Saga of Mid-
western Journalism.* Star-
Courier Press, 1947.

Leopold, Aldo. *A Sand County
Almanac.* Oxford University
Press, Inc., 1966.

Logan, Ben. *The Land Remembers: The Story of a Farm and
Its People.* Stanton & Lee, 1975.

Meine, Curt. *Aldo Leopold: His
Life and Work.* The University
of Wisconsin Press, 1988.

Mollenhoff, David. *Madison: A
History of the Formative
Years.* Kendall/Hunt Publish-
ing Co., 1982.

Martin, Lawrence. *The Physical
Geography of Wisconsin.* The
University of Wisconsin Press,
1965.

Monona Landmarks Commis-
sion. *City of Monona: Its
Landmarks And Heritage.*
City of Monona, 1980.

Paul, Barbara and Justus. *The
Badger State: A Documentary
History of Wisconsin.* Wm. B.
Eerdmans Publishing Co.,
1979.

Ridge, Martin, Editor. *Frederick
Jackson Turner: Wisconsin's
Historian of the Frontier.* The
State Historical Society of
Wisconsin, 1986.

Salkin, Philip H. *The Prehistory
of Dane County: A View of
12,000 Years.* A report for the
Dane County Regional Plan-
ning Commission, 1984.

Sprague, Paul E., editor. *Frank
Lloyd Wright and Madison:
Eight Decades of Artistic and
Social Interaction.* Elvehjem
Museum of Art, University of
Wisconsin-Madison, 1990.

Stegner, Wallace. *Where the
Bluebird Sings To the Lemonade Springs: Living and Writing in the West.* Penguin
Books, 1992.

Thayer, Crawford B., editor. *The
Battle of Wisconsin Heights.*
Crawford B. Thayer, 1983.

University of Wisconsin News
and Information Service. *University of Wisconsin-Madison
Almanac 1993.* Office of Peri-
odicals, 1993.

Wolfe, Linnie Marsh. *Son of the
Wilderness: The Life of John
Muir.* Alfred A. Knopf, Inc.,
1945.

Left: *A birdie's eye view?*
Below: *The green of Madison and Dane County.*

Above: *Budding pro.* ZANE WILLIAMS PHOTO
Top: *Bascom Hill.* JEFF MILLER/UW-MADISON
NEWS SERVICE PHOTO
Left: *Memorial Union Terrace.* JEFF MILLER/
UW-MADISON NEWS SERVICE PHOTO

Index

Algozin, Bruce 78–81, *79*
American Family Insurance 43
Atkinson, Gen. Henry 30–31
Attig, John 11–17

Barnes, Rev. Craig 85
Bascom Hill 6, 20, 21, 46, *109*
Belleville 73
Belzer, Dr. Folkert 52
Berry, Wendell 17, 79
Bishop, Andrew 64
Black Earth 4, 64–65, *67*
Black Earth Creek 4
Black Hawk War 28, 30–31
Black River Falls 26
Blue Mounds *3*, 4, 62–64
Blue Mounds Road 63
Bridge Road 26
Brigham, Ebenezer 28, 63
Brigham, J.R. 63–64

Cafe Europa 18
Callif, Linda 82–85
Cambridge 72
Camp Randall Stadium. *See*
    University of Wisconsin
Capitol. *See* Wisconsin State
    Capitol
Capitol Square *33*; description 6,
    18–21; history 28, 40; pictured
    8, 75, 86, 94
Carpenter, Mary 74
Cave of the Mounds 64
Child, Ebenezer 37
Children's Museum 21
Christ Presbyterian Church 85
Clayton, Lee 11–17
Clinton, Bill 56
Conover, Allan D. 52
Cooksville 73
Cottage Grove 69
Cows on the Concourse 45, 89
Cronon, William 10–11, 53

Cross Plains 4
CUNA Mutual Insurance Group
    43

Dairy industry 45
Dane County 7, 62–73, *64*
DeForest 69–70
Derleth, August 68
Doty, Judge James 28, 29, 32
Durand, Janice *87*, 88–92

Effigy Mound Tradition culture
    25
Elvehjem Art Museum 89
Emerson, Dick 69
Erdman, Joyce 96
Erdman, Marshall 61, *90*, 92–97
Evinrude, Ole 72

Farmer's market 9, *18, 19*, 74
Farming 45, 62, *101*
Featherstonaugh, George W. 6–7
Fish Hatchery Road 80
Four Lakes 25
Fox Indians 25
Funseth, Harvey 73

Gale, Zona 52
Gee, Alex *83*, 85–88
General Casualty 43
Glaciation 11–17
Goose Pond Sanctuary 70–72
Gore, Al 56
Grace Episcopal Church *18*, 82
Green Bay Lobe glacier 14

Hamilton, Mary Jane 61
Hamilton Street 20
Haraszthy, Agoston 69
Hegg, Colonel, statue of 20
Historical Society. *See* State
    Historical Society of Wisconsin
Hopkins, Steve 4, 76–78, *78*

Ideal Bar 81
Indians: Early Paleo- 24–25; Fox
    25; Sauk 25; Winnebago 25
Inn on the Park 57
Isthmus 18, 24, 29–32, *55*

Jackson, Jesse 56
Jamieson, Hugh 70
Javid, Manucher 52
Johnstown Moraine 14
Jolliet, Louis 68

Khorana, H. Gobind 52
King Street *37*
Kosta's (restaurant) 57

LaFollette, Robert Marion 53–
    56, *56*
Lake Mendota: description 21;
    geology 11; in history 28, 30;
    mentioned 6, 9; Paddle and
    Portage race 41; pictured *11,
    59*
Lake Monona *27*, 28, 41, *83, 90*
Lake Waubesa 25
Lake Wingra 48, *105*
Lake Yahara 14, 24
Leopold, Aldo 53, 99
Library Mall 48
Lincoln School 88
Lindbergh, Charles A. 49
Little Norway 64
Logan, Ben 9
Lower Wisconsin State Riverway
    68
Lynse, Per 72
Lyon, Orson 28

McCarthy, Sen. Joseph: on
    Frank Lloyd Wright 60
Madison, city of: pictured *5, 25*
Madison Civic Center 21, *23, 95*
Madison General Hospital 80

Madison, James 32; Memorial High School 10
Marquette, Father Jacques 68
Mazomanie 65
McFarland *71*
McGovern, Gov. Francis 56
Memorial Union *21, 23*
Memorial Union Terrace *2*, 21, *22*, 48, *109*
Meriter Hospital 42
Midvale Boulevard 96
Mifflin Street 20
Military Ridge Trail 64
Mills, Simeon 36
Mollenhoff, David 7, 39, 42
Monona 26, 28, 42
Monona Terrace Convention Center *61*
Mound-building Indians 25
Mount Horeb *62, 63*, 64, *67*
Muir, John 14, 52

Nakoma 34
Nehemiah Corporation 85
Nine Springs Marsh 25
Nobel Prize 48, 52

Observatory Drive 7
Oscar Mayer 44
Outboard Marine Corporation 72

Paddle and Portage race 41
Pail and Shovel Party 49
Paraskevoulakos, Gus 57
Peck, Eben and Rosaline 34–36
Peck, Rosaline *36*
Phelps, Richard 98–102, *100*
Philleo, Dr. Addison 30
Picnic Point 21, *46*, 48
Pinckney Street 20, *40*
Plizka, Bill 57
Prairie du Sac 25
Puzzlebox, The 92

Pyle, Tom 44

Ragstock *21*
Rayovac Corporation 44
Regassa, Markos 44–45
Rockdale Union Stoneware 72
Rowe Pottery Works 72
Rusch, Harold 52

St. Mary's Hospital Medical Center 42
Sand City *31*
Sand County Almanac, The 53, 99
Sauk Indians 30–31
Schmitz, Bob 40
Schubert's (restaurant) 64
Seely, Ron *112*
Sense of place 7–14
Signature Lounge 57
Soglin, Paul *100*, 102–103
Spring Green 52
Stanton & Lee Gallery 20
State Historical Society of Wisconsin 21, 39
State Street 6, *19*, 20, *29*, 42
Steenbock, Harry 49
Stegner, Wallace 17, 79
Stoughton *71*, 72
Sun Prairie 4, 36, *70*, 70–72
Sun Prairie Sweet Corn Festival 72
Suydam, J.V. 29
Syttende Mai festival *71*
Syverud, Pat 69

Taliesin Architects 61
Tenney, H.A. 7
Tenney Park *15*, *97*
Transitional Housing, Inc. 82
Turner, Frederick Jackson 10, 53
Tyrol Basin ski area *62*, 64, *94*

Union Tabernacle Church of God in Christ 85
Unitarian Church 60
University of Wisconsin: as employer 42; Badgers *50*; Camp Randall Stadium 49, *50*; establishment 39; history 46–53; location 6, 20, 21; Paddle and Portage race 41; pictured *26*, *47*; William Cronon 10
University Research Park 48

Vera Court apartments 103
Verona *95*
Veteran's Museum 21

Wakefield, John 30
Washington Avenue *41*
Waunakee 69
Wengler, Johann B. *37*
Williamson Street 6
Winnebago Indians 25
Wisconsin Dells 26
Wisconsin Folk Museum 64
Wisconsin Geological and Natural History Survey 11
Wisconsin historical society. *See* State Historical Society of Wisconsin
"Wisconsin Idea" 56
Wisconsin River *31*, *66*
Wisconsin State Capital 42, 53–57
Wisconsin State Capitol 6, *35*, 46
Wisconsin State Journal 76, 77
Wollersheim Winery 69
World Dairy Expo 45
Wright, Frank Lloyd 52, 60–61, 93, 96, 97

Yahara Place Park *12*
Yahara River *71*

About the Author

Ron Seely, 40, has lived in Madison for 15 years where he works as a reporter for the *Wisconsin State Journal*. For several years he wrote news and features from throughout the state, including breaking stories about everything from tornadoes to murders. For the past five years, he has specialized in project reporting, including an investigation of the state's aging public schools and an in-depth series about Bill Clinton's presidential primary campaign in Wisconsin. He lives with his wife and two children on the city's west side in a house that sits atop the high shoulder of a glacial moraine. In his spare hours, Seely haunts southern Wisconsin's trout streams, lakes, marshes, and woodland trails.

Dane County paradise.